TIME
MANAGEMENT
from the
INSIDE OUT

TIME
MANAGEMENT
from the
INSIDE OUT

The Foolproof System for
Taking Control of Your Schedule—
and Your Life

JULIE MORGENSTERN

AN OWL BOOK

HENRY HOLT AND COMPANY • NEW YORK

Henry Holt and Company, LLC
Publishers since 1866
115 West 18th Street
New York, New York 10011

Henry Holt® is a registered trademark of Henry Holt and Company, LLC.
Published in Canada by Fitzhenry & Whiteside Ltd.,
195 Allstate Parkway, Markham, Ontario L3R 4T8.

Library of Congress Cataloging-in-Publication Data

Morgenstern, Julie.
Time management from the inside out: the foolproof system for taking control of your
schedule—and your life / Julie Morgenstern.—1st ed.
p. cm
"An owl book."
Includes index.
ISBN 0-8050-6469-9 (pbk.)
1. Time management. I. Title.
HD69.T54 M66   2000
650.1—dc21   00-044983

Henry Holt books are available for special promotions and
premiums. For details contact: Director, Special Markets.

First Edition 2000

Designed by Carla Bolte
Figure art by M&M Design 2000

Printed in the United States of America

10 9 8 7 6 5 4 3 2 1

Dedicated to the memory of my father-in-law,
Gerardo Colon, whose unconditional love and goodness
filled my life, and will always inspire me to make time
for the people I love

CONTENTS

PART THREE : STRATEGIZE

PART FOUR : ATTACK

Introduction

TIME
MANAGEMENT
from the
INSIDE OUT

INTRODUCTION

The Power of Time Management

I was not always an organized person. In my first book, *Organizing from the Inside Out,* I shared the story of how I struggled with clutter and time management my whole life, and reached my turning point when my daughter was born. When she was three weeks old, she awoke from a nap on a beautiful summer day and I knew it was a golden opportunity to take her for her first walk. Unfortunately, it took me two and a half hours to gather supplies for our outing: blankets, bottles, pacifiers, diapers, toys, a sweater, booties . . . where were they all??!! By the time I was ready to go, she had fallen fast asleep. I had missed the moment. Disappointed and deflated, I looked down at my innocent babe asleep in her crib and thought, If I don't get my act together, this child will never see the light of day.

And so I conquered the chaos, starting first with the diaper bag and eventually tackling every other area of my home, office, and life. In the process, I discovered that organizing is not a mysterious talent but rather a completely learnable skill. I had just been going about it backward: I'd been diving into the piles instead of starting with a plan. I learned that by investing a little bit of time analyzing and strategizing beforehand, I could design a system that would last.

About three years later, I founded my company, Task Masters, a service that helps people get organized so that they may lead more gratifying lives. My staff and I provide one-on-one organizing services and seminars to thousands each year. My work with clients who come from all age ranges, genders, and personality types has enabled me to deepen my understanding of the organizing process and develop my emphasis on customizing the solution to each individual. In 1998 an editor at Henry Holt and Company asked me to write a book on my techniques. The result was my first book, *Organizing from the Inside Out,* which has become a *New York Times* best-seller.

Fourteen years after that diaper-bag fiasco, I was given the opportunity to see just how far I'd come with my organizing skills. Less than two weeks before my daughter's Bat Mitzvah (a huge affair that, as a single parent, I had coordinated by myself), I got the call every author dreams of—it was from the Oprah Winfrey show. They wanted to fly me out to organize their offices as well as several viewers' homes for their big "Spring Clean-up" show . . . all within the next ten days!

Was I ready to jump on this fantastic opportunity without hesitation? Was I organized enough to manage all of the details involved in pulling off both the Bat Mitzvah and the *Oprah* show simultaneously? The answer was a resounding *yes!* Because I was more organized, most of the details regarding the Bat Mitzvah were done. What wasn't done was written on a list, and I could do a quick scan to see exactly where I stood. My planning and delegation skills came in very handy—I was able to prioritize the tasks and decide what my staff and friends could do in my place. My files and database were very organized, so any information I needed for either event was at my fingertips. And during the whirlwind of the next two weeks, my planner kept me very focused on everything I had to do and every place I had to be. I didn't miss a beat.

My suitcase was packed in a flash and I was on the next plane to Chicago. Instead of missing the moment, I was able to embrace this unexpected convergence of priorities. The result was one of the most glorious weeks in my life—celebrating a momentous, spiritual occasion with my daughter, and appearing on the most coveted TV show in the world. Here's to the power of time management!

Being organized, whether with your space or time, is all about being *ready*. It's about feeling in command so that you are prepared to handle all of the opportunities, distractions, and surprises life throws your way. We live in a complex, fast-paced world filled with infinite possibilities and opportunities. When you develop good time-management skills, instead of being overwhelmed by it all, you can celebrate it. You know what to choose. You feel clear and focused, ready to take on life.

If you haven't yet read my first book, *Organizing from the Inside*

Out, I encourage you to do so. It was designed to be a primer in the process of organizing. In the journey from chaos to order, it is often easier to start with space organizing, because it is much more tangible than time. Furthermore, once you organize your space, you will have much more time on your hands to manage. (Most studies show that we lose an average of one to two hours per day searching for missing items in messy files, closets, and stacks.) But whether you have read *Organizing from the Inside Out* or not, you will find *Time Management from the Inside Out* very valuable.

When you use the time-management techniques discussed in this book, you will take control of your days. You'll feel content and happy about how you spend your time. You will maintain a balance between work and love and play that energizes you and makes your life feel rewarding. You will learn how to tune in to yourself, and consistently spend your time in ways that are meaningful to you.

HOW THIS BOOK IS STRUCTURED

This book is divided into four parts:

Part 1: Laying the Foundation. This section will revolutionize the way you think about time and set you up to begin creating your own time-management program.

Part 2: Analyze: Tuning In to Who You Are. This section takes you through a series of questions and self-tests that help you define your personal style, preferences, needs, and goals so that you will be able to customize your time-management program.

Part 3: Strategize: Designing a Life You Love. This section helps you map out your ideal schedule and select the tools to keep you on track.

Part 4: Attack: Making It Happen. This section shows you how to put your plan into action, and maintain control while dealing with the realities of everyday living.

Although you have to make some mental shifts in perception and learn some new skills, I will not ask you to change who you are in order to conform to a rigid program. The program outlined in *Time Management from the Inside Out* honors you and your unique goals, and allows you freedom and flexibility. So let's get to it!

PART ONE
LAYING THE FOUNDATION

I

A WHOLE NEW WAY OF LOOKING AT TIME MANAGEMENT

So what makes time management so difficult? It is my observation that the single most common obstacle people face in managing their days lies in the way they view time. Therefore, the very first step in taking control of time is to challenge your very perception of it.

MAKING TIME TANGIBLE

Most people think of time as intangible. In the journey from chaos to order, it is often easier to organize space than time, because space is something you can actually see. Time, on the other hand, is completely invisible. You can't see it or hold it in your hands. It's not something that piles up or that you can physically move around.

Time is something you *feel,* and it feels . . . utterly amorphous. Some days go whizzing by, others crawl painfully along. Even your tasks seem hard to measure—infinite and endless in both quantity and duration.

As long as time remains slippery, elusive, and hard to conceptualize, you will have difficulty managing your days. You need to change your perception of time and develop a more tangible view of it. You need to learn to see time in more visual, measurable terms.

In my own journey to getting organized, my biggest breakthrough came when I realized that organizing time really is no different than organizing space. Let's compare a cluttered closet to a cluttered schedule to see the similarities.

Cluttered Closet	Cluttered Schedule
• Limited amount of space	• Limited amount of hours
• Crammed with more stuff than storage	• Crammed with more tasks than time
• Items jammed into any available pocket of space, in no particular order	• Tasks jammed into any available pocket of time, in no particular order
• Haphazard arrangement makes it difficult to see what you have	• Haphazard arrangement makes it difficult to see what you have to do
• Inefficient in its use of organizing tools	• Inefficient in its use of time-management tools

In other words, just as a closet is a limited space into which you must fit a certain number of objects, a schedule is a limited space into which you must fit a certain number of tasks. Your days are not infinite and endless. When you think of it this way, time is not so intangible and elusive. In fact, each day is simply a container, a storage unit that has a definite capacity you can reach.

Once you understand that time has boundaries, you begin to look at your to-dos much differently. Tasks are the objects that you must fit into your space. Each one has a size, and arranging them in your day becomes a mathematical equation. As you evaluate what you need to do, you begin to calculate the *size* of each task and whether you can fit it into the space.

When you start seeing time as having borders, just as a space does, you will become much more realistic about what you can accomplish, and much more motivated to master various time-management tools and techniques to help you make the most of your time.

If a cluttered closet and a cluttered schedule are the same, then organizing each is a very similar process. My first book, *Organizing from the Inside Out,* taught that whether you are organizing a closet, kitchen, office, or schedule, designing a system that lasts lies in always following the same three steps: ANALYZE–STRATEGIZE–ATTACK.

This book is a thorough examination of how the three

steps of the organizing process apply to the particularities of time. Throughout, we will build upon this more tangible view of time, and show you how to arrange your schedule just as you would a beautifully organized room, one that reflects what's important to you. It will be easy to figure out where your time goes, and to find time for the important things in your life, because every activity and task will have a "home."

DEFINING TIME MANAGEMENT FROM THE INSIDE OUT

Time management from the inside out is about designing a schedule that is a custom fit for *you*. It's about identifying what's important to you and giving those activities a place in your schedule based on your unique personality needs and goals. And it's about feeling deeply satisfied at the end of each day.

Time Management from the Inside Out honors and celebrates the fact that everybody is different. And each of us has different needs at different points in our lives. There is no "right" way to live your life. I am not here to tell you to live a simple, calm life, nor to convince you to fill every waking moment with highly productive activity. Nowhere in this book will you read "truisms" such as "the early bird catches the worm," or that you must work less, or play less, or be anything other than who you are.

Instead, this book will help you tune in to who you are and what you want, and then give you the tools to build your life around that. You can learn new skills and modify some behaviors, but you can't really change your essence—and you shouldn't. This book will take you through a process of self-discovery of your likes and dislikes, natural habits, needs, and desires. These become the foundation of your time-management system. My system offers you a process, not a prescription.

The following two profiles illustrate how completely different one person's life can look from the next, and yet both can successfully manage their time from the inside out.

Patrice: Structured, Predictable, and Calm

Patrice is a thirty-eight-year-old married mother of a four-year-old boy. She works full-time as a senior staff writer for a woman's fashion magazine. She thrives on routine, enjoys a sense of calm, and hates to feel rushed or pressured. Her family and personal time are just as important as her work time, and keeping a balance between them all is extremely important to her.

Patrice is very clear on her goals: she wants her son to feel loved and important, she wants to keep her marriage well nurtured, and she wants to maintain her reputation as a highly dependable, talented writer.

She wakes her son every morning at 6:45 and they go through a delightful morning routine, which includes singing songs while he gets dressed, having breakfast, and playing a game before they walk to his school. After dropping him off, she knows she needs a little transition time to go from "mom-head" to "work-head." So each morning she goes down into the subway and lets four trains pass while she reads *The New York Times*. She hops on the fifth train and arrives at work focused and ready to go.

Her workday also is filled with routines. She writes in the mornings, and researches, interviews, and attends staff meetings in the afternoons. She checks her planner to see exactly what she needs to do and gets right to it, without hesitation. She has never missed a deadline.

She works 9:30 to 5:30 five days per week. She picks her son up from school three days per week, but has her mother or her husband pick him up on Mondays and Thursdays. This frees her up to work late every Monday night, and see a friend for a movie on Thursdays. Patrice delegates well. She believes strongly that including others in the care of her son not only keeps her life in balance, but also enriches his life by surrounding him with many people who love him.

Weekends have a predictable pattern, too. Friday nights are family video night. Saturday mornings she takes Kyle to a music class, and in the afternoon they eat lunch at a local restaurant and then go to the playground or a museum. Every Sunday Patrice's husband and Kyle have their own father-son outing, while Patrice stays home to prepare for her upcoming workweek.

Patrice pays astute attention to how long tasks take to do and pares back her schedule so that she has ample time for each activity. She's calculated how long it takes her son to get dressed every morning, and wakes him up in time for him to get ready at his pace. Patrice's life is built solidly around her priorities, and is delightfully predictable, calm, and gratifying to her. It's a life that fits her personality and priorities, is rich and rewarding, and is built for her from the inside out.

Andrew: Work-Centered, Fast-Paced, and Unpredictable

Andrew is fifty-six and the CEO of one of the world's largest resort chains. He thrives on variety, loves interacting with lots of people, and is a highly creative problem solver. He doesn't need much time to "stew" on things. He is quick on his feet, confident in his opinions, and focused. He can shift gears easily, handling interruptions well.

Andrew is passionately committed to his work, and his goal is to keep his company on the leading edge. His mission is to set an example of extraordinary customer service every day, pursue all significant opportunities for growth, and study as much as he can about his industry.

Andrew's time is structured to support and celebrate his personality and goals. His days are structured to allow for a lot of spontaneity and variety. He is at his desk every morning at seven and spends the first hour reading industry journals, then spends one hour handling e-mail and phone calls. From nine o'clock on, his time is left open to handle all of the needs, urgencies, and requests that come up all day long in running a large corporation. Andrew keeps a very short to-do list. He knows his job is to respond to the needs of others and having a long to-do list would only frustrate him. In between meetings he keeps going back to his desk to answer calls and e-mails. His mission for the past thirty years has been to answer every phone call (and now e-mail) the day it comes in. He has met that goal. At the end of each day (which ends somewhere between six and eight P.M.), he spends one more hour at his desk, responding to the last of the phone calls and e-mails that came in.

Andrew delegates extremely effectively. He finds and hires the best talent to run the various departments of his organization. He works very closely with his secretary and they have many tools to support a fast-paced teamwork. They have designed checklists and forms for speeding up communication between them regarding travel arrangements, setting appointments, planning meetings, and adding "contacts" to one of his sixteen mailing lists. Their computers are networked so that both Andrew and Dorothy can easily access his online calendar, which Dorothy keeps for him.

All day long, Andrew responds immediately to the needs of the people who work for him. He rapidly works down the stack of papers in his in-box, dispatching each of them in seconds, jotting notes directly onto the paper or using one of his preprinted forms. He makes quick decisions.

Andrew works long hours—usually twelve-hour days—but he reserves evenings for dinners with his family and friends. He gets the bulk of his pleasure from his work—it is a source of tremendous energy for him. However, as much fun as he has at work, he knows the value of relationships outside work and time off. Weekends are his leisure time, and he enjoys taking regular vacations.

Andrew's life is rich and rewarding, and he too has built it from the inside out.

As you can see, Patrice and Andrew are very different people with very different ways of doing things. Patrice sticks closely to her highly determined framework each week, while Andrew's bare-bones framework allows for a lot of spontaneity. Yet they both feel great about how they are spending their time, attack each day with vigor and excitement, and feel satisfied at the end of each day.

Everyone would like to have as much control over their days as Patrice and Andrew do, but for many people, something is standing in the way. As you will see in the next chapter, it's important to know what is preventing you from being able to manage your time. Once you know what's holding you back, you can pinpoint the solution.

2

WHAT'S HOLDING
YOU BACK?

When people struggle to manage their time, they very often jump to the conclusion that they are internally flawed somehow, that they are born incompetent in this area of life. Or they throw thier hands up in resignation, convinced that "out of control" is just how life is supposed to be in the modern world. Both of these perceptions are totally inaccurate and self-defeating.

Once you learn the skill of diagnosing time-management problems, you will stop wasting time and energy beating yourself up or working yourself to exhaustion. You will simply run the problem through the following three-level diagnostic, accurately zero in on the cause, and get to work on the proper solution. Swift, clear, accurate. Now, that's a time-saver!

A Three-Level Diagnostic

- **Level 1: Technical Errors.** These are easily resolved mechanical mistakes. You need a skill or a technique you don't have, and this book will teach it to you. Once you understand these errors, you simply make the appropriate adjustments to your approach and you're all set. Problem solved.
- **Level 2: External Realities.** These are environmental factors that are actually beyond your control. You didn't create them, and they put a limit on how organized you can be. By recognizing these you can stop blaming yourself and find a more direct way to manage or eliminate them.
- **Level 3: Psychological Obstacles.** These are hidden, internal forces that prevent you from achieving the life you desire. If you have conquered all of your technical errors and external realities and are still feeling out of control, it's likely that you have a psychological force working against you. When you realize what's causing certain self-sabotaging habits, you can begin to break free of their control.

Often it's a combination of forces that create time-management problems. Consider all three levels of errors and obstacles when you are diagnosing what is going wrong. Otherwise, you may end up with a partial fix—you will remove the external reality that's preventing you from accomplishing certain tasks but the psychological obstacles will remain.

When you understand all the causes of your problem, you can create true change from the inside out. Each time you look at one of your time-management problems, ask yourself, "Is my problem technical or external or psychological?" For example, if you are having trouble delegating, is the problem technical ("I don't know how to do it"), external ("There's no one I can delegate this to"), or psychological ("I feel guilty asking someone else to do this for me")?

I suggest you reread this chapter whenever you get stuck, and ask yourself what's causing the problem right now. You may discover that there are certain obstacles that tend to cause problems for you over and over again. Ultimately you'll learn to recognize them when they surface, quickly diffuse them, and stop them from sabotaging your efforts to manage your time.

LEVEL 1: TECHNICAL ERRORS

Error #1: Tasks Have No "Home"

One of the most common reasons you may not be getting to things that are important to you is that you haven't set aside a specific time in which to do them. Too often, people make lists of *what* they want to do, without asking the next essential question: *When* am I going to do this? Unless a task has a "home," that is, a time slot clearly blocked out in your schedule, you won't get to it.

If you think you will get to anything in your "spare time," keep in mind that *there is no such thing as spare time!* As it is, our days are packed with more things to do than there will ever be time for. The only chance we end up with a free moment is when something we planned falls through at the last minute. Then, we usually can't think of what to do with those unexpected moments because we were caught off guard.

So if something is really important to you, set aside a specific time in your schedule to make it happen. You'll learn more in chapter 5, "Time Mapping," and chapter 9, "Assign a Home," about assigning a "home" for each task.

Error #2: You've Set Aside the Wrong Time

If you've set aside time to do something but find yourself still not getting to it, it's possible that you've set aside the wrong time. We all have energy and concentration cycles: Some of us are morning people, some of us are most energetic at night. Some of us feel motivated to begin big, new projects at certain times of the year, such as January, September (when we're in a back-to-school mind-set), or when the warm weather begins. Some women find that there are times of the month when they are better able to handle projects requiring focus or patience.

If you are working against your own energy or concentration cycles, it will be hard to effectively tackle a task when you've planned to. If you can't bring yourself to balance your checkbook each month as you promised yourself, maybe the problem is that you're always trying to do it at night after work, when your mental energy is low. If you schedule the task in the morning instead you'll probably find yourself more motivated to tackle those figures.

For more about working with your natural rhythms and energy cycles, see chapter 3, "Understanding Your Personal Relationship to Time."

Error #3: You've Miscalculated How Long Tasks Take

Most people are very unrealistic about what they can accomplish in a day. If the time required to complete your to-dos exceeds the time you have available, you simply won't get to it all and you'll end up feeling frustrated and demoralized. This is completely avoidable. If you get better at calculating how long tasks take, you can plan a realistic workload. Learning how to estimate how long tasks take is a skill anyone can learn, as you will see in chapter 7, "Sort." Furthermore, when you know what your big-picture goals are, it will be much easier to eliminate, shorten, or delegate tasks that don't serve your goals. Chapter 8, "Purge," will help you develop skills to solve the problem of more tasks than time.

Error #4: You're the Wrong Person for the Job

Too many of us make the mistake of thinking that we have to do it all, that asking for help is a sign of weakness. It can be hard to admit that when it comes to certain tasks, you're simply the wrong person for the job. But it can also be liberating. We all have unique talents and skills, and so do other people. It can save a lot of time, headaches, and heartaches to admit that someone else can do a job faster, better, and more efficiently than you. Maybe you have an assistant, or friends or family members, who would actually enjoy a job that's difficult and tedious for you. If someone else is better at balancing your checkbook or designing a new sales brochure, accept that, hire them, and move on.

You'll learn more about the art of delegating in chapter 8, "Purge."

Error #5: The Task Is Overly Complex

If you are not getting what's important to you, it may be that the way you are approaching the task is overcomplicated. If a particular chore is too complex and cumbersome, chances are you'll avoid it altogether. If you want to see success, you need to simplify the task.

Many people create filing systems that are far too complicated, consisting of hundreds of file folders with only one or two pieces of paper in each. Their filing eventually backs up because it's overwhelming to try to remember where each paper goes. By keeping your file headings broad, you'll have less options on where a piece of paper can go, and you'll be more likely to do your filing promptly. Similarly, it's easy to get overwhelmed by big projects. Maybe you want to organize your photographs, but you think you have to do the entire project in a single sitting, sorting through all fifteen years of backlog and placing them in albums in the proper order. A task this large can be so intimidating that it will cause you to procrastinate. However, if you break down the project into smaller steps it becomes manageable. You could buy photo shoe boxes one day. Do a general sort of photos by date the next day. Then tackle one box and one album a week until the project is complete.

Break complex projects into small steps and keep it simple. Chapter 8, "Purge," offers an entire section on creating shortcuts to simplify the routine tasks in your life.

Error #6: You Can't Remember What You Have to Do

If you don't have a single reliable to-do list or planner, chances are you won't get to many of your important tasks simply because you can't remember that you have to do them! This sounds overly simplistic, but in the busy, overstimulating environment we live in, it's hard to rely on memory alone. Even with the best intentions, we often get distracted and forget what we wanted to do. To avoid this, you will need to consistently record your to-do lists and appointments—including the appointments you make with yourself or your family—in one dependable place. Chapter 6 will help you pick a planner that works for you.

Error #7: Your Space Is Disorganized

Even if you are an otherwise excellent time manager, a disorganized physical environment will steal a huge amount of time and energy from your day. You'll waste hours searching for your keys, your reading glasses, or some important document. You'll work inefficiently, get stuck redoing lost work, and have to run out and replace items you can't find.

The *Wall Street Journal* reports that the average executive loses six weeks per year searching for missing information in messy desks and files. That breaks down to just one hour per day per person—a conservative estimate at best. *USA Today* reports that Americans waste 9 million hours every day looking for misplaced items.

The solution to this technical error is simple: Organize your space. The average office takes just three days to organize, the average room in a home takes one to one and a half days. This is a small investment against the gain of six or more weeks per year!

It's too overwhelming to organize everything all at once, but you can start with the room in which you spend the most time. The sooner you invest the time organizing, the sooner you will gain the extraordinary benefits of more time to work with. My first book, *Organizing from the Inside Out,* will teach you a simple, foolproof plan for taking control of any space in your home or office.

LEVEL 2: EXTERNAL REALITIES

External realities are situations in which you are faced with significant time-management challenges beyond your control. They have a profound impact on your ability to manage your time. When you recognize external realities you can get to the heart of the problem and figure out a way to adapt to them. This will allow you to take the blame off yourself and find a pragmatic solution.

External Reality #1: You Have an Unrealistic Workload

Sometimes an unrealistic workload is self-imposed due to technological errors or psychological factors. But other times the force does come externally and you just have to admit that life has overloaded you at the moment. Maybe you are working, going to school, and trying to raise children. Maybe your assistant at work just left, your computer crashed, or your home-renovation project has gone horribly awry and your to-do list is rapidly filling up with tasks you hadn't anticipated.

If you're up against any of these challenges, whether your

extenuating circumstances are short-term or long-term, you'll have to reexamine your workload and focus on self-preservation. Be kind to yourself. Get rid of extraneous tasks, streamline, and delegate them. Dramatically lower your standards for certain to-dos, just to keep your head above water.

Chapter 8, "Purge," will help you learn how to reduce your workload and depend on others during this tough time. Chapter 10, "Containerize," will help you adapt and adjust your plans and expectations during the extenuating circumstances. By following the program in this book, you will be able to create a custom time-management system for yourself that is flexible enough to accommodate these unexpected events and crises.

External Reality #2: A Health Problem Limits Your Energy

When we're not feeling our best, and our energy is flagging, it's very difficult to do everything we've set out to do. Some people have serious health disorders that put limits on their energy. You could be slowed down by clinical depression, or attention deficit disorder, or any of a number of health problems that you may not even be aware of. If you feel lethargic all the time, or find yourself always sleeping, you could have anything from a thyroid problem to sleep apnea to a nutritional deficiency. Check with your doctor and see if there's a medical problem you can address. Moreover, so many people are sleep-deprived—new parents, doctors and nurses, anyone who works a late shift or travels a lot. Don't underestimate how much this can sap you of energy as well as the ability to focus and do difficult analytical tasks.

And, of course, we all catch colds or the flu, but too many of us think we can still get to just about everything on our to-do list. Take care of yourself and work with your temporary or permanent health and energy problems. Chapter 5, "Time Mapping," will show you how to work *with* your energy levels instead of trying to ignore your limitations.

External Reality #3: You Are in Transition

When you're in transition, it's very hard to figure out how to spend your time. Your old system doesn't fit anymore, and you don't have a new system in place yet.

There are many transitional situations that can disorient you: marriage, divorce, birth, death, retirement, graduation, moving, a job search, a business merger, etc. When the structure of our lives changes, it can take time to adjust. We get used to doing things one way, then suddenly we have a boss who wants us to work less independently and check in with her all the time, or we are used to being able to sleep in after a long night's studying and now have to start a job at eight A.M. And when a life change suddenly frees up windows of time that were formerly occupied, it's not always easy to figure out exactly what we want to do with our newfound freedom.

When you're disoriented by a transition, identify your goals and try to create a new basic framework for yourself, understanding that it may change. Always start with one or two definite anchors, and build from there. For example, if your new boss needs you to report in regularly, set up specific times for mini-meetings with her. Then track how things go, and make adjustments until it feels right. Chapter 5, "Time Mapping," will help you create a framework that supports your goals.

External Reality #4: You Are in an Interruption-Rich Environment

The interruption-rich environment is a challenge for even the best time managers. A doctor can't control when his patients will need emergency care. Public relations people, real estate agents, stockbrokers, salespeople, and many others in service-based industries all have interruption-rich jobs that require them to be extremely responsive to others.

How do you handle an interruption-rich environment? By acknowledging and planning for it. Leave plenty of time for the interruptions and crises. Then create a little oasis of time for yourself that is totally under your control by putting your phone on voice mail, or asking a colleague to fill in for you, or waking up a little earlier each day.

Doctors often plan for fifteen minutes of paperwork time for every hour of patient work. They may need to save up this time to put in at the end of a very busy day—but they know they have to allow for this time and ask another physician to cover for them while they catch up. This oasis of time allows them to regain control without work piling up to mammoth proportions. If you're a new mom who is breast-feeding and sleep-deprived, you can catch up by napping when the baby sleeps and having someone else give the baby a bottle once a day so that you can have a few extra hours of uninterrupted sleep.

Also, if you spend a lot of time traveling or waiting, you can use this transit time as a "floating" oasis. Keep the work you want to do with you at all times, and whenever you get stuck in transit or waiting in line, jump on these moments to tend to the items on your to-do list.

Chapter 5 will teach you how to develop a Time Map that allows you to create these havens free of interruption, and chapter 8, "Purge," will help you learn to delegate.

External Reality #5: You Have a Disorganized Partner

What if you are living or working with somebody whose disorganized ways keep interfering with your own time-management plans? If there is anyone whose disorganization affects you on a regular basis—a chaotically driven spouse, child, boss, co-worker, client, or business partner—you'll need to resolve the conflict in order to eliminate your anger and keep the relationship healthy. If you can, get this person to work with you on improving his or her own time management. If you can't, you will have to negotiate a solution.

Remember that the best negotiations always start out by identifying the common goals you have with the other person. This will eliminate any defensive feelings and put both of you on the same side of the fence. With a boss, your common goal may be to produce the best widgets in the country. With a spouse, your common goal may be to create a harmonious home. Once the common goal is agreed upon, you can explain the ways in which you are personally investing your time and working to accomplish this goal. Your partner may actually disagree with your choice of efforts, in which case you can compromise on how to use your time most effectively. If your partner agrees with how you're using your time, you can then describe how their last-minute gear-shifting is working against your ability to achieve the shared goal. Then, as a team, you can brainstorm ways to prevent last-minute chaos.

You may not be able to solve the problem completely, but by talking about it and searching for the points of agreement you will eliminate resentment, and you can work as a team on the solutions. The key is to eliminate your feelings of being stuck or victimized so that you can create a life that is fulfilling and gratifying to you.

LEVEL 3: PSYCHOLOGICAL OBSTACLES

Sometimes we don't allow ourselves to improve our time-management skills to make time for what's really important to us because of psychological obstacles. We know what we need to do, but resist taking action because our time-management problems are serving us somehow—they are fulfilling some deep-seated need we may not even be aware of. Without awareness, these forces will sabotage your efforts to take control of your time. These psychological obstacles often don't reveal themselves until after you've conquered the technical errors and external realities. In fact, it's often best to deal with time-management problems on a very practical level first. Frequently, once you begin experiencing the benefits of managing your time from the inside out, many of the psychological resistances melt away.

If you have worked through the program in this book and still are having some trouble managing time, come back to this list and spend some time thinking about your own tendencies. Often, just realizing what you've been doing and why you might be doing it is enough to move you toward change.

While I'm not a psychologist and can't diagnose the root of any given psychological obstacle, in my years of hands-on practical experience in the organizing field I've discovered several types of psychological blocks that hold people back from managing their time as much as they would like.

Psychological Obstacle #1: You Have Unclear Goals and Priorities

Without clearly defined goals, you have no basis for making decisions on how and where to spend your time, or on how to prioritize and sift through the many choices that confront you on a daily basis. That's why it's so important to read chapter 4, "Developing Your Big-Picture Goals," and determine what your biggest priorities in life are.

I am convinced that most people know in their hearts what they want. The problem is that many childhood experiences and messages make us lose sight of or deny what we want, because somewhere along the line our goals were treated as inappropriate, impossible, or unimportant. Maybe as a child you had so many responsibilities piled on you that you got the impression that your own needs and wishes didn't matter, so you stopped paying attention to them. Or perhaps you had so many choices that you never learned to figure out what you really wanted.

No matter what experiences caused you to detach from your desires, your job is to find a way to reconnect to what makes you happy. Chapter 4 will help you.

Psychological Obstacle #2: You Are a Conquistador of Chaos

If you constantly keep your schedule packed beyond the scope of reality, if you always leave everything to the very last minute, and if your life feels like one urgent calamity after another, chances are you are a "conquistador of chaos." You set your life up to be in constant disaster mode because, quite frankly, you are a wonderful crisis manager. You feel so good conquering the impossible that you keep creating it, just so that you can rescue yourself. You pull it off every time—though not necessarily without some "fallout" along the way.

If you are a conquistador of chaos, chances are you got your training for this role when you were a child. Perhaps you were raised in a difficult environment where you were the organizer, peacemaker, or the problem solver. You learned to feel a certain comfort in crisis, and you felt good about your ability to handle chaos. Now your job is to learn how to feel good about that ability without having to test it on a daily basis. For advice on working with being a crisis manager, see chapter 10, "Containerize."

Psychological Obstacle #3: You Have a Fear of Downtime

For some people, "downtime" is very anxiety provoking. If this is you, the idea of taking a day off with nothing to do fills you with dread.

Maybe you feel guilty if you take time off and are not productive. Maybe you keep yourself in constant motion because you think others admire you for being so active. If so, you are probably locked in a cycle of all work with no rejuvenation time. This can lead to burnout.

You may actually be keeping your schedule packed and your mind cluttered so that you don't have time to think about larger, more difficult issues, such as what you really want to do with your life, or how to deal with unhappiness in your marriage. Be prepared for the fact that once you have a calmer schedule and time to think, you may have to begin dealing with matters you have been afraid to look at.

A profound fear of downtime can also be a clue of childhood trauma. People who were abused as children often find it very frightening to be alone with their thoughts. To avoid getting into these quiet situations, they sometimes develop the habit of chronic lateness. After all, if you are always late, you won't get stuck waiting . . . and thinking.

If you suspect that you are distracting yourself with busy-work to avoid an unpleasant task or issue, you may want to gather the courage to explore the issue further. But you don't have to rush this confrontation. In the meantime, give yourself permission to keep a very busy schedule. However, instead of filling it with "busywork," fill it with an activity that's meaningful for you. Plan to get to places early, but have something compelling to occupy your time while you are waiting. Schedule breaks from work, even vacations—but don't go hanging out on a beach. Fill them with activity—exercise, visits to the museum, movies, or sightseeing (see p. 217 for more suggestions on what to do during downtime). It's fine to keep yourself very busy, but make sure you are creating a balance of meaningful activities—including time for work, for play, for self, and for family.

Psychological Obstacle #4: You Need to Be a Caretaker

Helping other people can make your life rich and rewarding. And in fact, you can even choose to devote your life to serving others. Usually, such sacrifice is deeply gratifying but if this gets out of balance, it can cause you to feel resentful, unappreciated, and overwhelmed.

Before you blame the people around you, ask yourself if you are actually the one setting up this imbalance. Sometimes, we get so caught up in our own need to be appreciated and feel valuable that we don't let other people help us.

Maybe you are trying to replicate your memories of someone who was a wonderful caretaker in your life. Maybe you feel pride in being able to accommodate anyone who asks a favor of you. It feels good momentarily, but too many yeses and you can't follow through. Eventually, your good-natured inability to say no will hurt your reputation more than help it.

Remember that part of expressing love and concern for other people is allowing them the pleasure of helping out. You empower people when you allow them to contribute. Give yourself a break—and give the people around you a chance to grow.

See pp. 161–63 for advice on how to just say no.

Psychological Obstacle #5: You Have a Fear of Failure

If you know what your goals are, but are not getting to the things that are important to you, it could be that you are suffering from a fear of failure. It can be very frightening to go after your dreams, and find out you are incapable of achieving them. Sometimes it's easier to avoid making the effort, blaming circumstances or the fact that you didn't get to try, rather than experiencing the feeling of failure. You may feel that failure would be devastating.

It's so easy to overestimate how terrible failure will be. Sometimes just being honest with yourself about what's the very worst thing that can happen will help you overcome your fear. Then, too, if you think of failures as opportunities to learn, grow, and move closer to your goals, it may be easier to face down your fear.

Each time you fail, imagine yourself telling your life story on a talk show in ten years, or to your grandchildren someday, inspiring all the struggling dreamers out there about all the failures you experienced along the way.

Psychological Obstacle #6: You Have a Fear of Success

The achievement of our dreams can produce just as much anxiety as failure can. Being successful can make you stand apart from your family and friends. Going to college when your peers and friends are not can make you feel that you're growing away from them. Being promoted to a supervisor in charge of overseeing your friends at work can be very uncomfortable. Perhaps somewhere along the way, you were given the message that you don't deserve success. Once you recognize this fear of success, it's much easier to move through it. Everyone deserves success. If you have a fear of success, spend time with people you consider successful. It will demystify the scary aspects and make success feel within your reach.

Psychological Obstacle #7: You Have a Fear of Disrupting the Status Quo

Sometimes, you don't pursue your goals because you fear the reactions of the people around you—your boss may not like it, your kids may balk—because they're used to things the way they are. If you are afraid to disrupt the status quo, you may be forsaking what's most important to you for what is comfortable, safe, or secure. This is a variation on fear of success.

When you are fearful of change, remember that you may be able to make the change in such a way that it's more gradual and less wrenching. Taking small steps can give you and others a chance to get used to the change.

Psychological Obstacle #8: You Have a Fear of Completion

Some people have a hard time making progress toward their goals and getting through their to-do lists because they actually have a fear of completion. They keep starting projects, bouncing back and forth between all of them, yet have a hard time finishing any one of them. They never get to truly enjoy a feeling of accomplishment, and the result is a loss of energy and self-esteem.

Often people have a hard time finishing projects because they love the creative process and hate having to make a choice and close themselves off to all their other options. If this is the case, keep reminding yourself that there will always be new projects and new chances to enjoy the process of creating. It can be helpful to recognize that there are both a creator and an editor inside you. Once the creator has had a fair turn at the project, it's time to let the editor take over. Another technique is to spend time with people who love to get things done. Sometimes, through osmosis, you can learn to savor the joy of completion.

If you don't finish a project and it keeps lingering on, sometimes it's simply because the project is no longer important to you. Give yourself permission to let go of the time and effort you have invested. When you let go of the obsolete, you free yourself up for new projects.

Psychological Obstacle #9: You Have a Need for Perfection

If you're a perfectionist, you feel compelled to do everything at the same level of excellence.

Good time-managers keep things in perspective. They set priorities rather than give every task equal weight. If you demand extremely high standards for every single task you undertake, you simply won't get everything done.

The need for perfection often comes out of a need for approval. It could also come from a fear of criticism, humiliation, or harsh judgment. It could be that you grew up conditioned by a well-meaning teacher or a parent who drummed into your head, "If you're going to do things, do things right!" You didn't learn how to evaluate which tasks were worth a huge amount of exertion and which weren't. Or it could be that you feel more secure when everything seems to be under your control.

For your own sake, you need to adjust your standards based on the specific task at hand. Some tasks are worth your finest effort, and others just need to get done. For help in learning when enough is enough, see chapter 10, "Containerize."

Psychological Obstacle #10: You Have a Fear of Losing Creativity

Many creative or "right-brained" people fear that imposing structure in their lives will squelch their creativity or their free-spirited personality. As a result, their personal and business lives are chaotic and cause them tremendous stress.

If this is your situation, be assured that imposing structure can actually be liberating. Many of the most successful creative writers, artists, and musicians find great freedom in structure and discipline. They write or paint or draw at the same time every day. Some days the creativity flows, others it trickles out, but the consistency of their schedule assures that they make time for what is important to them.

Structure doesn't destroy your creative impulses, it allows them to flourish. After all, when your schedule is free-form, you often don't get to the things that are most important to you. Your creative work takes a backseat to the more urgent demands of other people, and you neglect your own needs, such as paying your bills and making doctors' appointments.

You need to learn to trust that you can put structure into your schedule and still have enough freedom to hear the call of your muse, or respond to opportunities that crop up, or spend time with your friends, customers, and associates. You don't have to plan every hour, but you can map out a general rhythm to your day.

If you are afraid of structure, *Time Management from the Inside Out* will work well for you because it will allow you to accommodate your natural behavior patterns. You can customize your schedule to work for you, as you will see in chapter 5, "Time Mapping."

Becoming aware of what has been holding you back can make a monumental difference in your effort to gain control over your time. Fortified with these new insights into why you act the way you do, you have a real head start in creating long-lasting change.

You are now ready to begin the process of managing your time from the inside out. The next stage is analyze, where you will look within and explore your personal relationship to time.

PART TWO

ANALYZE

Tuning In to Who You Are

3

UNDERSTANDING YOUR PERSONAL RELATIONSHIP TO TIME

"To thine own self be true."
—William Shakespeare

The first step on the journey to becoming a better time manager is to do an honest self-assessment. This evaluation will help you harness your strengths and will save you time by focusing your efforts on just those areas that need improvement. Perhaps most important, it helps you develop a deeper understanding of your unique relationship to time.

> I am such a procrastinator. I occupy my time with trivial matters and then rush in the final hours to do what's important. I want less stress and more pride in my life.
>
> *—twenty-five-year-old musician*

I make elaborate lists of things to do, but then I don't follow them. Sometimes I don't even remember that I prepared a list of things to do. I am always behind in all aspects of my life.

—*fifty-two-year-old real estate broker*

I am good at starting projects but get sidetracked easily. It's hard to stay focused on one thing at a time. Before I know it, the day is gone and I am left with the frustrating feeling of time lost and tasks not achieved. I want to reverse that.

—*forty-one-year-old mechanical engineer, married*

Balancing my life is so hard. I have a husband and three kids at home. I find I'm constantly changing hats all day from secretary, cook, laundress, chauffeur, you name it. I am soooooo tired at night, yet always feel guilty taking time off because there's still so much to be done.

—*thirty-one-year-old pastor's wife*

I never get anywhere on time. I try to pack way too much in before going anywhere or I procrastinate prior to leaving. This creates a lot of pressure, yelling, and embarrassing situations for myself and my kids.

—*forty-year-old homemaker, married, four kids*

While many people feel frustrated with the way they are managing their time, each person's specific issues are different. By examining your unique time-management experience, you will learn a tremendous amount about yourself.

Buried under the chaos and confusion of your days are clues about your individual strengths and weaknesses, personality style and preferences, your unique sources of energy, and what makes you happy. By tuning in to your individuality now, you begin the process of custom-designing a solution that will be a true match for who you are.

In exploring your personal relationship to time, we will examine three areas:

1. What's Working and What's Not
2. Your Time-Management Preferences
3. Your Energy Cycles and Sources

WHAT'S WORKING?

No matter how out of control your life may seem, there are always some things that work for you in addition to the long list of things that do not. It is invaluable to start by looking at what works. First of all, it will boost your self-confidence—no doubt, a lovely way to begin a journey. You will inevitably discover that you have a base of some time-management skills, even if they are only "selectively applied" at the moment. When you've discovered these skills, you can begin to build on them in other areas of your life.

Identifying what's working will save you an enormous amount of time and energy because, clearly, there is no need to fix what isn't broken. It will also provide critical clues about what appeals to you—information that will help you fix all the areas that aren't working.

Let me give you an example.

Gina was a freelance computer consultant who felt she had a

split personality when it came to time management. Whenever she had an appointment with a client, she got there precisely on time, was energetic and focused throughout the session, and was consistently able to get a tremendous amount done. Yet on the days when Gina was in her own office, doing administrative or business-related duties, she was highly unproductive. No matter what was on her to-do list (bill paying, writing proposals, strategic planning), she'd find herself procrastinating, wandering around, reading through the junk mail, taking phone calls, and frittering the day away. As a result, her business (and self-esteem) were suffering.

When I asked Gina why her time with clients was so much more productive, she came up with two reasons: One was that Gina found contact with people very energizing; the other was that Gina was very responsive to the structure of the appointments. With a well-defined start and end time, Gina explained, she was able to focus and pace herself to make sure she made the most of the time allotted. So how could she apply this insight to address what wasn't working?

On her days in the office, I suggested she assign start and end times to each of the items on her to-do list. For example, she'd write "Draft new brochure 10:00–10:45 A.M.," "Filing 12:00–12:45 P.M." directly in her planner. In addition, I recommended that she break up her solitary tasks with people contact. Following every forty-five minutes of concentrated work, she'd make a couple of phone calls to re-energize herself. She also scheduled lunches with clients, prospects, vendors, or friends on "office days" as an added reward and break. This combination of creating appointments for her to-dos and interspersing contact with people fueled Gina's energy and made her productivity on "office days" soar.

Think about what's working for you. This can be a free-form exercise, or you can use the sentence starters below to help get you started. You may want to type your answers on a computer or write them in a notebook with a lot of room for answers. Think long and deep about these questions, and consider all the areas of your life—work, home, relationships, personal growth, etc.—when answering.

EXERCISE 1: WHAT'S WORKING?

Fill in as many answers to the following questions as you can think of:

No matter how busy I get, I always find time for_____.

My goals are well defined when it comes to_____.

I'm pretty clear on how long it takes me to_____.

I never procrastinate about_____.

I am never late for_____.

I have no problem exercising when_____.

I have no problem tackling difficult projects when_____.

I always build in transition time between_____.

It's easy for me to say no to_____.

Meeting deadlines is easiest for me when_____.

I am at my happiest when I am_____.

The things that I delegate easily are_____.

Sample answers:

"No matter how busy I get, I always find time to <u>read to my kids at night, clean out my fridge, see new clients, get the invoices out, etc.</u>"

My goals are well defined when it comes to <u>my kids, my work, my marriage, etc.</u>

I'm pretty clear on how long it takes me to <u>walk to work, get dressed in the morning, shave, cook dinner, write a speech, go food shopping, design a proposal, etc.</u>

I never procrastinate about <u>feeding the baby, gardening, paying the mortgage, eating dinner, writing in my journal.</u>

I am never late for <u>the airport, a dinner date, client appointments, the movies, doctors, etc.</u>

I have no problem exercising when <u>I first wake up, am on vacation, am watching TV, have company.</u>

I have no problem tackling difficult projects when <u>it's Monday morning, I have enough lead time, my kids are not around, it involves other people, etc.</u>

I always build in transition time between <u>work and home, one creative task and another, working with numbers and playing with my kids, etc.</u>

It's easy for me to say no to <u>requests for volunteering, my mother-in-law, unreasonable demands, working overtime, etc.</u>

Meeting deadlines is easiest for me when <u>the deadline is set by someone else, I'm under pressure, it comes to money, at work, etc.</u>

I am at my happiest when I am in my garden, brainstorming new ideas, dancing, surfing the Internet, etc.

The things that I delegate easily are the laundry, data entry, taking out the trash, copyediting, legal work, etc.

Now, look over your answers and see what you can learn about yourself. Ask yourself why these particular things are working. Are you getting to certain tasks because you enjoy them so much? Or because you are very skilled at them? Are you responding to outside pressures ("If I don't do it, I'll get fired, so I always get it done") or inside pressures ("If I don't do this, I won't be happy with myself")? Does it have to do with the time of day that you choose to do them, or the amount of time each one takes? Are you better at doing solitary tasks than collaborative ones? Ask yourself what makes these things work.

Even if some of the areas that are under control in your life seem trivial, they can help you figure out how to fix other, bigger problems. Jane was a high-powered lawyer, with a husband and three kids, who was always overwhelmed with her to-do lists and suffering from burnout. The one task she always seemed to find time for was cleaning out the refrigerator. When I asked her why, she said that cleaning out the fridge was therapeutic. It was a purely physical task that was very gratifying because the results were so tangible (unlike a lot of the mental work she did as a lawyer and a mom, which produced such intangible results). It was a thirty-minute escape that seemed to recharge her in a way that doing the crossword puzzle just didn't do. Once she saw this connection, she realized that exercise (something she never took time for) would give her a similar result—it was a purely physical activity that would refuel her for the constant mental stress that predominated her life. She began scheduling thirty-minute power walks at her lunch hour and found her energy at work and at home heightened and enhanced.

WHAT'S NOT WORKING?

Now that you've seen that you actually are managing at least some of your time well and have some clues as to why, it's time to ask the next question: What's not working? The answers to this question may come more easily to you; after all, it's what's not working that motivated you to read this book in the first place.

Still, it's helpful to write your responses down and take a look at the whole picture. It will be interesting to compare your answers to this question to your answers to the What's Working questionnaire.

Again, this can be a free-form exercise, or you can use the following sentence starters to help get your thinking started. Remember to consider all the areas of your life when answering.

EXERCISE 2. WHAT'S NOT WORKING?

Fill in the blanks. Think of as many examples as you can.

I never have time to_____.

I spend way too much time on_____.

I don't have well-defined goals for_____.

One thing I wish I could do every day is_____.

I always underestimate how long it takes to_____.

I procrastinate whenever I have to_____.

I am usually late for_____.

It's hard for me to say no to_____.

I have a hard time finishing_____.

Here are some sample answers:

I never have enough time to exercise, relax, see my friends, prospect for new business, make follow-up calls, etc.

I spend way too much time cleaning the house, filing, processing e-mail, attending meetings, etc.

I don't have well-defined goals for my personal life, my career, my finances, etc.

One thing I wish I could do every day is play my guitar, exercise, nap, talk one-on-one with my kids, eat a sit-down lunch, etc.

I always underestimate how long it takes to write a proposal, shop for groceries, review reports, plan a meeting, organize my closets.

I procrastinate whenever I have to start a new big project, pay bills, exercise, make collections calls.

I am usually late for work, appointments, the dentist, everything.

It's hard for me to say no to my boss, my kids, my spouse, persistent people.

I have a hard time finishing the laundry, letters, the dishes, big projects, the photo album project.

Your answers to this question become your list of everything you want to fix. In this book, you will learn how to address all of these problems. Every so often, come back to this list and see how much progress you've made toward reaching your goals.

But before moving on, take a good look at this list and compare it to your list of "What's Working?". If you are having trouble starting or finishing certain tasks and not others, ask yourself why. In some cases, things aren't working because you need to develop certain skills, such as preventing interruptions or calculating how long tasks take. Or you may simply need to apply a skill from one area of your life to another.

For example, James owned a delicatessen, and due to the long hours of his business, he never seemed to have time for his household chores. The pressure of tasks undone was constantly eating away at him, and he resented spending his few hours of time off on menial, though necessary chores. His "What's Working?" list revealed that he had no trouble delegating duties to his staff at work. He'd even hired his teenage nephew to run chores for him in his deli, and found the arrangement extremely effective. Upon thinking about it, he saw that he was able to delegate at work so effectively because he had written out instructions and created simple forms for basic procedures. He realized that he could do the same thing for many of his home-related tasks. By writing out instructions and creating simple checklists, he was able to delegate many of his household chores as well, both to his children and to hired help. This freed his time off to be just that.

YOUR TIME-MANAGEMENT PREFERENCES

Sometimes you struggle with some tasks more than others not because you're lacking a skill, but because of individual preferences or the particular conditions under which those tasks occur. Whether you know it or not, we all have preferences about when and how to do certain tasks or activities. When we honor those preferences, it's easier to get things done. Tuning in to these natural inclinations can help explain why certain items are landing on your "What's Working?" and "What's Not Working?" lists.

To help you discover the preferences and natural inclinations that affect whether or not you get to certain tasks and activities, do the following exercise. Obviously, there are always variations in our preferences, but think about your first instinct in answering these questions, how you feel *most* of the time.

EXERCISE #3: YOUR TIME-MANAGEMENT PREFERENCES

On a piece of paper, write out the following list and circle your preferences.

The majority of the time, I prefer. . . .

Working independently	vs	Working collaboratively
Exercising alone	vs	Exercising with others
Relaxing alone	vs	Relaxing with others
Concentrating in short bursts	vs	Concentrating for long stretches
Focusing on one thing at a time	vs	Multi-tasking (doing more than one thing at a time)
A fast and busy schedule	vs	A slow and easy schedule
Plans and predictability	vs	Surprises and spontaneity
Tight deadlines	vs	Long lead times
"Stewing" on things	vs	Making quick decisions
Working in silence	vs	Working with background noise or music
Dim lighting	vs	Bright lighting
Working with my head	vs	Working with my hands

There are no right or wrong answers to these questions, although some people might try to convince you that there are! What is important about your answers is that they may provide further insights into your What's Working? and What's Not Working? lists. This information will help you plan a schedule that delights you. For example, if you thrive on a fast pace, you will know to fill your day with many activities. If you prefer a slow pace, you may limit your daily to-do list to three to four items.

Too many people don't think to consider their natural tendencies, and end up with a schedule that works against them.

YOUR ENERGY CYCLES AND SOURCES

In addition to your natural preferences, the ups and downs of your energy can have a profound impact on your effectiveness at tackling certain things on your to-do list. Energy is power; it is what enables you to move toward your goals. Once you recognize and understand your natural energy sources and cycles, you can begin to manage them. Without being tuned in, you may be trying to tackle your most challenging activities when you're feeling sluggish and wasting your peak energy on less demanding tasks.

Long days, a lot to do, pressure, eating on the run—all these can contribute to flagging energy. So can heat, humidity, monotony, boredom, dim lighting, staring at a computer screen for hours, jet lag, sleep deprivation, and certain medications. Some of these are an inescapable part of life in the twenty-first century, but avoid known energy drains when you can. When you can't, counter them with a potent energy booster.

Since you can't always control when you do certain tasks, the best time managers are also very tuned in to what activities fuel their energy when it is flagging. This varies from person to person, so you need to think about what works for you. By knowing what energizes you, you can avoid energy drops throughout the day altogether and fully enjoy whatever you are doing, whether it's work or play.

Explore your own natural body rhythms and energy boosters by answering the following questions.

EXERCISE #4: IDENTIFYING YOUR ENERGY CYCLES
AND SOURCES

Part 1: Write down your answers to the following questions.

Mornings are the best time for me to_____.

  And the worst time for me to_____.

Afternoons are the best time for me to_____.

  And the worst time for me to_____.

Evenings are the best time for me to_____.

  And the worst time for me to_____.

Late at night is the best time for me to_____.

  And the worst time for me to_____.

Part 2: Circle the answers that are true for you. Then think about whether there are other answers to this key energy-management question.

When my energy is flagging, I can usually recharge by:

- changing activities
- exercising
- stretching
- playing some music
- reviewing my goals
- glancing at a photo of someone I love

- drinking a glass of water
- taking a catnap
- eating a high-energy snack
- taking a brief break
- planning something fun
- calling a friend
- other

Sometimes, a change of pace is all you need to boost your energy levels. If you have been concentrating for hours and your brain needs a break, it's a great time to do a task that requires you to move around and use your muscles. Similarly, if you have been doing mindless physical tasks all day, your body may need a break, but your brain may be raring to go. Do a mentally stimulating task. When you've had a lot of social activity, maybe it's time to schedule a quiet task, and vice versa. When you plan your day, make sure you build in enough variety to keep yourself invigorated.

———

The key to *Time Management from the Inside Out* is to build your life as much as possible around your individual needs and desires. Does this sound unrealistic? I promise it isn't. Once you've developed some basic time-management skills—and anyone can master them—you will have much more control over your daily, weekly, and monthly schedule. Then you will be able to factor in your energy levels, your preferences about pace and interruptions, and your energy ups and downs. And even when you cannot impact your environment, it is helpful to know what your optimum is, so that you can quickly identify what's working against you and compensate for it.

As you refashion your approach to time, you'll discover all kinds of interesting and wonderful things about yourself. Time management is the ultimate in self-improvement, because it is the foundation that will enable you to achieve your goals in every aspect of your life.

What if you don't know what your goals are? Then you need to define them clearly. The next step in the process of self-discovery is to articulate clearly what you want out of life. In the next chapter, you'll learn how to clarify what your big-picture goals are.

4

DEVELOPING YOUR BIG-PICTURE GOALS

What's it all about . . . Alfie?

—*Burt Bacharach/Hal David*

In today's fast-paced world, it's so easy to get lost in the details: the daily demands on your time, the endless chores and tasks that make your head spin. Does this sound like your life?

Too much to do, I don't know where or how to start. I feel as though my wheels are spinning at 100 mph and I'm getting nowhere fast.

—*forty-seven-year-old real estate broker*

I want to be in control. I don't like a rigid routine, but I would like the satisfaction of knowing that I'm using my time effectively and that I'm making progress. Sometimes it gets so bad that I don't even want to think about what needs doing for fear of feeling overwhelmed!

—*thirty-five-year-old IT trainer, divorced, with three kids*

I write little notes to myself about things to do, projects to work on, ideas for my writing. All of these notes just accumulate in little piles.

—*forty-nine-year-old consultant/writer, married, with no kids*

It seems like I am always cleaning, and never getting anywhere. I always feel guilty spending time with the kids because I know more has to be done. And the house is always a mess!

—*thirty-one-year-old homemaker, married, with three kids*

When life becomes about the million and one things on your to-do list, you lose perspective. You have no easy way of deciding between one thing and the next because it all seems equally important and urgent. It's also nearly impossible to feel a sense of satisfaction because no one ever gets to everything on the to-do list. So you end each day exhausted, depleted, and dissatisfied, feeling that you didn't do enough. Even if you got a lot done, you feel aimless, as if it were all for nothing, because you're still overwhelmed with things you feel you must do.

No matter how hectic life gets, the most successful people are able to rise above the chaos and keep their perspective because they have what I call big-picture goals. The big picture is your overriding vision of what your life is all about and what you want it to be. When you can see the big picture, it's easier to do tasks you dislike, because you understand how each task fits in with your life goals.

Your big-picture goals give meaning, motivation, and direction to your life. They make it easier to cut tasks from your to-do list when you run out of time while still feeling good about your day. Therefore, the next step in your journey to being a better time manager is to develop your big-picture goals.

WHAT IS YOUR MOTIVATION?

Why are you reading this book? Yes, you want to become a better time manager, but you want to do that because it will allow you to achieve a *higher* goal. Managing your time better will enable you to accomplish something vitally important to you. Ask yourself what that something is.

Before writing this book, I conducted an informal Internet survey and asked visitors to my Web site why they wanted to become better time managers. Out of 1,500 survey responses, over 70 percent of respondents said what they wanted was to find *more* time. What varied was what they wanted the extra time for:

I want to accomplish mundane tasks more quickly and easily so I have more time to spend with my friends, more time to work on craft projects, more time to have fun.

—twenty-four-year-old administrative assistant

I want more time to talk one on one with my kids.

—thirty-six-year-old stay-at-home mother of four

To gain time for personal enjoyment—reading, listening to music.

—nineteen-year-old graduate student

I want to have more discipline and be able to accomplish things. My lack of time management means that I am not accomplishing any of my goals in life, such as learning new skills, getting in shape, taking classes, and above all, finishing my Ph.D. so I can get a real job.

—thirty-one-year-old social worker

To stop and smell the flowers, instead of trampling over them in a mad rush to be somewhere I should have been an hour ago.

—forty-eight-year-old physician

There were other reasons as well:

I want peace internally—a sense of satisfaction at my accomplishments rather than constant frustration.

—twenty-eight-year-old freelance journalist

To project a better image to my boss and co-workers so that I can get a promotion.

—thirty-two-year-old insurance adjuster

To be able to feel like I can take time to do things I know I need to be doing for ME everyday (spiritually).

—forty-year-old homemaker and mom

To have a clue about what's coming up next.

—fifty-seven-year-old payroll manager

Write down your own compelling reason for becoming a better time manager, and keep it close by. It will provide a starting point for a more highly developed set of big-picture goals for each area of your life. It will also help you stay motivated as you go through the journey of learning time management. Whatever your reason, remember that although it can be challenging to change ingrained behaviors, when you focus on all you have to gain, it's easier to succeed.

GOALS, ACTIVITIES, AND TASKS

You picked up this book because there are vitally important things you want to do, and you're not getting to them. Life is flying by, and you are feeling rushed, stressed, or frustrated. Time management from the inside out is about identifying what's important to you—your big-picture goals—and making changes in your behavior that allow you to achieve your desires.

There are three tiers of defining the life you want:

1. Developing big-picture goals
2. Selecting activities to help you achieve those goals
3. Choosing the daily tasks/to-dos that make up your selected activities

Part Three of this book will help you figure out and sort through the tasks you will have to perform as part of your activities. Before you get to that, however, you will need a clear vision of the big picture and what your activities will be.

DEVELOPING BIG-PICTURE GOALS

Your dreams and desires are the heart of time management from the inside out. I wholeheartedly believe that you can accomplish just anything you want when you set your mind to it. When you look at the big picture of life and think about what you want, you get in touch with your deepest values and think about the fundamental things that will make you happy. And once you know what is really important to you, you can work toward achieving those goals.

Your big-picture goals will be simple and general rather than specific: warm and loving relationships, well-adjusted kids, financial security and wealth, expertise in a particular area, an inviting and comfortable home, a sense of connection to your community, and so on. You don't have to think about the *how* to get what you want. All you need to say is *what* you want in the broadest terms. When you actually articulate your big-picture goals, you take the first and extremely significant step toward realizing them.

It's essential to consider your deepest values and identify your big-picture goals for every major life category that's meaningful to you. Many of my clients set career or financial goals, but neglect to set goals for other critical areas of their lives. If your life feels out of balance, look to see where you are spending the majority of your time. Chances are that your time is being spent in those areas of your life for which your goals are clear. To feel nourished, energized, and balanced, you need to set big-picture goals for all the significant categories of *your* life. What are the major departments of your life? Possible categories to consider are:

- Work
- Family
- Self
- Romance
- Friendship
- Finances
- Knowledge
- Home
- Spirituality

The categories you choose might look a little different from these. Maybe at this point in your life Friendship or Romance isn't important to you. Maybe you think of Knowledge as part of Self or Home as part of Family. Feel free to create a list of categories that reflects what is important to you using wording that makes sense to you.

Now look at your major life categories and ask yourself, "What would make me happy in these key areas of my life?" Think *big* (you can determine what are unrealistic goals later). When all is said and done, what are you doing on this earth, and what do you need to feel that your life is worthwhile and satisfying? What do you dream of having, being, and doing?

I believe that all of us at our core know what would make us feel joy and contentment, but many of us are afraid to give ourselves permission to achieve what we really want. You deserve happiness. Don't edit and judge yourself. Just dream!

Write down one or two big-picture goals for each major life category. You might think of these as mini–mission statements. For family, Diane wrote: "I want a home that is a warm, inviting place for my family to live and to spend time with friends." Terrence's big-picture family goal was: "To make my kids feel really loved and important." For work, Alan, a caterer, chose: "I want to be recognized as the most innovative caterer in the city." Jill, a lawyer who wanted to reduce her hours at work to spend more time with her kids, selected: "I want work that nourishes me, while leaving me time to nourish my children." Pauline's big-picture relationship goal was: "To make sure my husband always knows how happy I am I married him." Maria's big-picture knowledge goal was: "To become an aficionado of theater."

If You Are Having Trouble Defining Your Big-Picture Goals

Are you having trouble articulating your goals?

Frankly, I believe that at your core, you really do know what they are.

In *The Magic of Thinking Big,* David J. Schwartz wrote that we dream of what we want to do, but few of us surrender to our desire. Instead, we murder our dreams with self-deprecation, "security-itis," and other "murder weapons." Schwartz says that success requires heart-and-soul effort, and we can put our hearts and souls only into something we really desire. If you have "murdered" your dreams to the point where you feel you can't even identify them, there's good news. You haven't actually murdered them; you've just knocked them unconscious. You can revive them. One of the best ways to tap into what makes you happy is simply to observe yourself very closely by creating a "joy journal." Throughout the day, whenever you notice you have just done something you've enjoyed, jot it down in your journal. Start paying attention to what delights you. Those activities are usually indicators of what makes you happy at your core and can bring you closer to the discovery of your goals. Give yourself permission to love what you love—whether that is cleaning out your refrigerator, reading poetry, or painting your kitchen.

Periodically review your joy journal and see what you learned about yourself. For example, one entry may be "Beth called today with boyfriend problems, spent an hour on the phone helping her figure out what to do. Loved feeling useful and helping a friend." What goals might come from this? Perhaps you will decide that you enjoy problem solving or counseling. Maybe these activities should be a part of your work, and maybe you need to make more time for them in your life.

Maybe you feel you are so far away from where you would like to be that you can't allow yourself to acknowledge your dreams. If it's hard for you to define openly what you want out of life right now, try thinking ahead to the distant future.

THE TEN-YEAR GAME. Visualize your life ten years from now. If you could have anything you want, fantasize what your life would look like. Paint a picture in your mind of your ideal job, home life, and social life. Don't worry about reason or logic. Your fantasies should be loose and free—the grander, the better, as long as they sound wonderful. You've got ten years to get there; the pressure's off. Be bold!

Once you have the picture of your future in your mind, divide a piece of paper into two columns. On the left, list each of your major life categories. On the right, write what you are doing. You might write:

- Self: "I am traveling extensively."
- Family: "I am married to someone I love, and I will have three children."
- Work: "I will be running my own business."
- Friends/Relationships: "I have friends who add to my life rather than having friends who are a drain on my energy."
- Finances: "I have a huge investment portfolio."
- Community: "I live in a small town where I am surrounded by friendly, caring people."

Are you able to visualize what your life will look like in all its aspects? There's no reason not to achieve these goals and realize your dreams.

"ONE FOR NOW." Sometimes it's hard to define your goals because you have so many interests and desires. How can you narrow your choices? You want to improve your computer skills, learn to play tennis, start your own business, decorate your home, get your doctorate in engineering, and write your novel—all this while working full-time and raising your three kids. Everything is appealing, so it's hard to give up any of your wonderful options. You can't choose any goals because that would mean eliminating some of the others. But because you can't focus, you're not actually *doing* any of these fabulous things.

Try the "One for Now" exercise, to help you focus. Make a list of *all* the things you want to do. Sing at Carnegie Hall. Travel to Greece. Have three kids. Buy a house. Work for an international consulting firm. Write down everything that appeals to you.

Give yourself permission to want what you want. If you judge your dreams as they come out, you'll be too intimidated to continue to express yourself. Don't worry about what is possible yet, just dream, and dream big.

Now pick one goal to achieve for now. Bear in mind that you can add any of the others in at any time. You can change your mind about this if you discover along the way that's not really what you want. Remember that by picking one, you are *not* eliminating your other goals. You are simply getting started toward one of your goals.

WRITE DOWN YOUR GOALS. I strongly recommend that you write down your big-picture goals. In a well-known study of the Yale class of 1953, the recent graduates were questioned about their future plans. Only 3 percent had written out their goals and plans of action. Twenty years later, this 3 percent appeared happier and more content than the others; furthermore, this small group had achieved more wealth than the remaining 97 percent of their classmates put together.

When you put your goals in writing, almost as if by magic, opportunities to realize your dreams begin to present themselves to you. Some people explain this by saying you begin to *attract* what you need. I don't think this is how it works. I believe we are surrounded by opportunities to achieve almost anything we want every day of our lives. But it's all a big blur. Once you have written down your goals, you begin to *notice* the specific opportunities in your path that will help you get where you want to go. Clarity of goals produces clarity of vision.

Once you have written your list of goals, review them often. Post them in your office or carry around a copy of them in your purse or wallet. Keep them in the front of your mind; it will help you stay focused and give you a much greater likelihood of success.

Jack Canfield and Mark Victor Hansen, authors of *Chicken Soup for the Soul,* set a tremendously ambitious goal of selling 1.5 million copies of their first book in a year and a half. Each of them wrote the goal on an index card and reviewed it a minimum of four times a day. Did they achieve their goal? In eighteen months, they sold 1.3 million. Pretty darn close. Danielle Steele had a twenty-five-year goal of selling 500 million books; she made it.

DETERMINING YOUR ACTIVITIES

Once you know what your big-picture goals are, you need to determine a few specific activities that will help you to achieve those goals. Unlike big-picture goals, which tend to stay the same year in and year out, the activities you choose to accomplish those goals will change as needed. They may change annually or more often, as you move closer to your goals, accomplish what you set out to do, or discover a better path to your goal.

If your goal is to challenge yourself intellectually, you might choose activities such as going back to school, reading a book a week, or attending lectures and seminars at least once a month. If your goal is to build wealth, you might choose to develop a budget and cut expenses, or learn about the stock market so that you can begin investing in it—or find an investment adviser.

Take each big-picture goal and make a list of some activities you can do over the next year or two that will get you there. Be as specific as possible. Here is an example of how your list might look.

Major Life Category	Big-Picture Goal	Specific Activities
Self	Maximize health	• Get more sleep • Exercise three times a week • Eat home-cooked meals
Family	Warm, welcoming home	• Daily pickup of clutter • Weekly cleaning • Decorate
	Well-adjusted kids	• Daily one-on-one time • Help with home-work • Weekly family out-ings
Work	Fulfilling career	• Improve skills • Job hunt • Network

Major Life Category	Big-Picture Goal	Specific Activities
Relationships	Exciting marriage	• Daily talks with spouse • Weekly dates • Private weekends away
	Solid friendships	• Weekly talks • Write e-mails • Monthly get-togethers
Finances	Build wealth	• Invest 20% of each paycheck • Read the *Wall Street Journal* • Learn to invest • Pay bills on time
Community	Make a contribution	• Volunteer at a shelter • Donate clothing and food

You may have trouble determining *how* to pursue one or two of your goals. For example, you may want to start a home-based business, but you don't know what it will take to make that happen. In that case, your specific activity may be to do research on this project. You may choose to read some books on the topic or log on to the Internet and ask other small-business owners how they got started.

Another problem you may run into is that you generate so many activities that you can't begin to pursue them all. For instance, your list may include eight things to do to develop a fulfilling career, ten steps to build wealth, and fifteen ways to make your children feel loved. If you have more than three or four activities in any category, you will overwhelm yourself and throw your schedule out of balance. Focus on the top three or four choices in each category and postpone the rest. You'll need to keep it simple so that your schedule stays in balance.

Revise Your List of Activities Annually

As I said, your big-picture goals will rarely change because the things you value will tend to remain constant throughout your life (for example, you may always want solid friendships, well-adjusted children, and financial security). However, the way you strive toward your big-picture goals will change regularly. You will replace some of the specific activities you've chosen from year to year as you achieve some of your smaller goals and outgrow other activities. You may find it feels natural to reevaluate your activities at particular times of the year—in January, as the new year begins; in September, when you're in a back-to-school mode; or, if you live in a cold climate, in the spring, when the warm weather and sunshine return and energize you to start planning new projects.

Changes in your life circumstances also can affect which goals you emphasize at different times in your life. When your kids are young, their well-being may take precedence over your career fulfillment. Once you have built wealth, you may choose to spend more time on activities related to self-fulfillment.

Once a year, reevaluate your activities. For each big-picture goal, ask yourself, "How will I pursue this goal this year?" If one of your goals is to have a warm, welcoming home, here is how your specific activities might evolve from year to year.

BIG-PICTURE GOAL: WARM, WELCOMING HOME

Year	Activity
Year 1	• Organize main living space and closets
	• Develop routines for maintaining clutter-free home
	• Keep house clean; hire housekeeper to clean once a week
Year 2	• Tackle attic, garage, and basement
	• Adapt family cleaning routines to accommodate new family schedule (youngest child goes to kindergarten, husband working fewer hours, etc.)
	• Begin hosting club meetings at our house twice a month
	• Redecorate first floor
Year 3	• Remodel kitchen
	• Host dinner parties twice a month
	• Build deck
Year 4	• Landscape front and sides of house
	• Plant vegetable garden in back of house

For some people, the process of defining goals can be eye opening, forcing them to focus for the first time on what they really
want in life. But for most people, it's less a surprise than it is a
process of clarification. You probably already had a pretty good
idea of what your goals are, even if it was rather vague, so it's likely
that the actions you have chosen to pursue here were ones you
were somewhat aware of before now. In fact, you are probably already engaged in some of these activities, but you may be surprised that there are many you aren't getting to. When you
develop and work with a Time Map, you can solve that problem.
You'll have designated times for your activities, and when you look
at your to-do list it will be clear when you are going to get to all
those tasks.

By doing the exercises in these last two chapters, you've already
made an important investment in yourself. With the knowledge
you have gained, you are well on your way to designing a custom
system that will help you achieve your ultimate goal of creating a
life you love. You're ready to move on to "Strategize"!

PART THREE
STRATEGIZE

5

TIME MAPPING

Creating Your Ideal Balance

We all have so much we want to do, and it's hard to keep track of time. Doesn't it seem that one department of your life takes over, causing you to neglect other vital areas?

Achieving balance means dividing your time into the right proportions for *you*. To make sure you leave enough time for the activities that support your personal big-picture goals, you will need to make a Time Map, that is, a schedule template that helps you achieve *your* ideal balance. *The Time Map is simply a visual diagram of your daily, weekly, and monthly schedule.* But it's also a powerful tool for helping you be proactive amid the swirl of demands that come your way. Instead of feeling that you have to act on every request the minute it crosses your path, you can glance at your Time Map, determine when you have time for this unexpected task, and either schedule it or skip it.

The Kindergarten Classroom Model of Organization

In *Organizing from the Inside Out,* I introduced the concept of using a kindergarten classroom as a model for organizing *anything*.

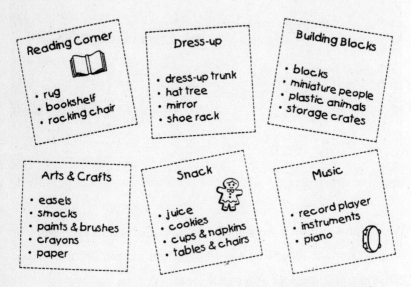

THE KINDERGARTEN MODEL OF ORGANIZATION

The reason a kindergarten classroom operates so well is that it's divided into clearly defined activity zones so that the children can focus on one activity at a time. There is a reading corner, an arts-and-crafts area, a music corner, and a dress-up zone. Items have clear homes, so there is only one logical place to find anything or put it away.

It's easy to see how you might apply this principle to any physical space, whether it's your kitchen or your office, but how does it apply to time management?

Your schedule's activity zones keep all your related tasks together: reading and sorting mail, e-mail, and phone messages, for example. Just as your shoes have a clearly defined home in your closet, tasks have a clearly defined home in your schedule.

When you set aside zones for each category of activity, it also prevents activities from spilling over into others, and ruining your ability to concentrate and enjoy the moment. Let's say it's Tuesday night, and you're playing Monopoly with your kids. When you land on Park Place your daughter says, "Pay up," reminding you that you have real bills that need to be paid. Instead of immediately rushing to get your checkbook, you think back to your Time Map. You know that you pay your bills on Saturday mornings, so there's no point in worrying about them on Tuesday nights. You can get back to your kids with a clear mind. Your Time Map is going to eliminate a lot of stress.

YOUR TIME MAP'S ACTIVITY ZONES

A Time Map is a schedule that is subdivided into "activity zones" that correspond to your life categories and contain all the tasks on your to-do list. As you will recall from chapter 4, your list of life categories looks roughly like this:

- Self
- Family
- Work
- Romance
- Finances

- Community
- Knowledge

All your activities will support your goals in these categories. For example, for the knowledge category, you might create an activity zone for taking a French class and another for studying. For the self category, you might separate relaxation time from self-improvement time: one day, your relaxation time is spent meditating by the lake and another day it's spent surfing the Internet; one day your self-improvement time is spent riding your bike, another it's spent working out to a video. *Do not focus on the specific task for now*. You can decide later whether you'll spend your relaxation time meditating or surfing the Net. The key is to have a set time for your chosen activities that helps you meet your goal of personal relaxation—and knowing which activity zone any given task fits into (which you will learn about in chapter 7, "Sort.")

Here are the Time Maps of three people who lead very different lives. Notice how the amount of time spent on any given category of activity varies from person to person.

William is a CFO of a major manufacturing company. His map is on page 83.

Samantha is a nurse and a mother of two. Her map is on page 84.

Erin is an entrepreneur and marathoner. Her map is on page 85.

Your Time Map may look very different from anyone else's, but the basic tool works for everyone.

TASK MASTERS

ORGANIZING AND TIME MANAGEMENT PROFESSIONALS
(212) 544-8722

⏱ Time Budget ⏱

Time	Monday	Tuesday	Wednesday	Thursday	Friday	Saturday	Sunday
6:30 A.M.	Wake Up	Wake Up	Wake Up	Wake Up	Wake Up	Wake Up	Wake Up
6:30 -	SELF—Shower, dress, breakfast					SELF— Writing autobiography	FAMILY— spirituality, church
7:00 A.M.							
7:30 -	SELF—Writing autobiography						
8:00 -	Commute, reading						
8:30 A.M.	WORK—e-mails						
9:00 -	WORK—internal meetings, calls				Sign checks		
12:00 P.M.	SELF—lunch/gym						
1:30 -	WORK—external meeting, offsite appts				↑	FAMILY— games, shopping, kids events	FAMILY— fun-day
5:30 -	WORK—e-mails, calls, daily tie-up				ROMANCE dinner w/wife		
6:30/7:00 P.M.	COMMUTE—Knowledge—Business reading			↑			
7:30 -	FAMILY—dinner, homework w/kids, family evening w/kids						FAMILY—knowledge, quiet time, reading at home (board mtg 1x/mo)
9:00 -							
9:30 -	ROMANCE—marriage-time			↑		ROMANCE— date night	
11:00 P.M.	Sleep	Sleep	Sleep	Sleep	Sleep	Sleep	Sleep

WILLIAM'S TIME MAP

SAMANTHA'S TIME MAP

⏱ Time Budget ⏱

Time	Monday	Tuesday	Wednesday	Thursday	Friday	Saturday	Sunday
6:30 A.M.	Wake Up	Wake Up	Wake Up	Wake Up	Wake Up	Wake Up	Wake Up
6:00 - 8:00 A.M.	FAMILY—wake, dress, play w/kids before school					SELF—sleep late	SELF—sleep late
7:30 - 8:00 A.M.	FAMILY—take kids to school						
8:30 - 10:30 A.M.	SELF—sleep or gym						
10:30 - 1:30 P.M.	FAMILY—clean, cook dinner for kids, errands, paperwork				pay bills	FAMILY—kids classes, practice, shopping	FAMILY FUN DAY— kids choice
1:30 P.M. - 2:00 P.M.	COMMUTE to work / FRIENDS—talk on phone						
2:00 P.M.	WORK—hospital						
10:00 P.M.							
10:00 - 10:30	COMMUTE to home / FRIENDS—talk on phone						
10:30 - 11:00 P.M.	FAMILY—tuck kids in, read before bed						
11:00 P.M. - 1:00 A.M.	SELF/KNOWLEDGE—read, watch news, unwind					FAMILY— stay at home— video night	FAMILY—quiet time homework, help, and check-up
1:00 A.M.	Sleep	Sleep	Sleep	Sleep	Sleep	Sleep	Sleep

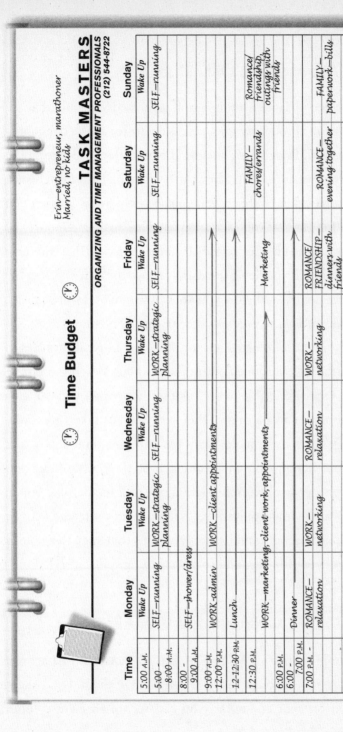

Time Budget

TASK MASTERS
ORGANIZING AND TIME MANAGEMENT PROFESSIONALS
(212) 544-8722

Erin—entrepreneur, marathoner
Married, no kids

Time	Monday	Tuesday	Wednesday	Thursday	Friday	Saturday	Sunday
5:00 A.M.	Wake Up	Wake Up	Wake Up	Wake Up	Wake Up	Wake Up	Wake Up
5:00 - 8:00 A.M.	SELF—running	WORK—strategic planning	SELF—running	WORK—strategic planning	SELF—running	SELF—running	SELF—running
8:00 - 9:00 A.M.	SELF—shower/dress						
9:00 A.M. 12:00 P.M.	WORK—admin	WORK—client appointments →					
12-12:30 P.M.	Lunch						
12:30 P.M. 6:00 P.M.	WORK—marketing, client work, appointments →			→	Marketing	FAMILY— chores/errands	Romance/ friendship, outings with friends
6:00 - 7:00 P.M.	Dinner						
7:00 P.M. 10:00 P.M.	ROMANCE— relaxation	WORK— networking	ROMANCE— relaxation	WORK— networking	ROMANCE/ FRIENDSHIP— dinners with friends	ROMANCE— evening together	FAMILY— paperwork—bills
10:00 P.M.	Sleep	Sleep	Sleep	Sleep	Sleep	Sleep	Sleep

ERIN'S TIME MAP

WHY TIME MAPS WORK

As you can see, a Time Map is a well-organized schedule that accommodates all of your activities, just as if it were a closet containing your belongings. Imagine an organized closet: the shoes are in the shoe bag, the sweaters are in a bin, the hats are hanging from hooks. If you get a new pair of shoes, you can see right away whether you have room for them. If you don't, you will have to create more shoe space—buy another bag, or get rid of another pair—so that your new purchase will fit. If you just haphazardly shove the new shoes in behind the sweater boxes, before you know it your closet will be disorganized and you'll waste precious time trying to find things in it.

Similarly, in order to manage your time, you must always aim to put new tasks into the zones where they belong. When something comes up, you will be able to see right away whether you can easily fit it into your plans or whether you have to take time away from another activity to make room for it. If you cram a new task in anywhere, hoping you will still get everything else done, you will soon find yourself running late again and feeling like you're not getting to the important things. Think of your selected activity zones as the containers and baskets and bins that keep the various categories of your life separate so that nothing spills over.

HOW TO CREATE YOUR TIME MAP

The first step in creating a Time Map is to sketch out what your activities are right now so that you can analyze them. On a sheet of paper, or on your computer (you can set up an eight-column table on Word for Windows), create your own blank Time Map. Write the days of the week across the top of the page, and the hours of the day in the left-hand column. Start your schedule with the time you wake up in the morning, and end with the time you go to sleep at night. Include your regular mealtimes. Write down your regular meetings, appointments, and classes.

Then, for a week or two, keep notes on what you are doing hour to hour, or if that's too inconvenient, note when you change activities. If your workday is nine to five and you go back and forth all day long between dealing with the public, performing administrative duties, and attending meetings, try to note generally when you're doing which type of activity. If you find you don't do any activity for more than a few minutes before switching, that's a good sign that your Time Map is going to help you a lot!

If your activities overlap—going to church with your family would be a family-time activity as well as a religion-time activity—note that, too. You probably have already figured out how to successfully combine some activities.

After a week or two, sit down with your current Time Map and take a long look at this snapshot of your life. How balanced is it? How much time are you devoting to each *type* of activity? Coloring in the blocks of time—yellow for family, blue for work, etc.—may help you see the answer even more clearly. Are you spending far too much time on one activity (such as watching television) or type of activity (relaxation time)? Maybe you're devoting several hours a week to administrative work and virtually none to marketing your business. Are you still spending time on activities that you've outgrown? Maybe you don't need to have so many meetings

A BLANK TIME MAP

⏱ **Time Map** ⏱

TASK MASTERS

ORGANIZING AND TIME MANAGEMENT PROFESSIONALS
(212) 544-8722

Time	Monday	Tuesday	Wednesday	Thursday	Friday	Saturday	Sunday
	Wake Up	Wake Up	Wake Up	Wake Up	Wake Up	Wake Up	Wake Up
	Sleep	Sleep	Sleep	Sleep	Sleep	Sleep	Sleep

at work now that interoffice communication has improved. Do you see pockets of free time that you tend to fritter away? Knowing when these pockets tend to occur, and how long they last, will help you plan a way to fill them with meaningful activity. Or are your days so tightly packed that it gives you a headache? Ask yourself if your schedule feels balanced.

Now that you know what your starting point is, you can start adjusting your Time Map to be in sync with your values and desires.

Creating an Ideal Time Map

In chapter 4, you defined your big-picture goals and identified the specific activities that support these goals. You will need this information to proceed, because now you are going to block out regular time zones in your schedule for all the activities that are important to you.

If your current Time Map showed that you were giving short shrift to self time, then you'll need to build more of it into your Time Map. Do you have enough relaxation time or alone time built into your days? If one of your personal goals is to play your cello at least four hours a week, and you haven't created regular time for that, now's the time to do so. You might schedule a large two-hour time block twice a week, or you could play for one hour at a time on four separate days.

While most of us have regular work hours, we don't have regular hours for our other activities. After you've figured out how much time you need to allot for them, you'll have to decide when to schedule them. Think back to chapter 3, when you learned about your energy rhythms. Then you'll know whether it's best for you to work out at the beginning of the day, or the end.

Within any activity zones, you might create smaller, more specific zones. At work, you might want to designate a specific time each day for returning phone calls and e-mails, and another block of time for meeting with your colleagues to exchange information. Within your big block of family time on the weekend, you could include chores and errands that help you meet your family goals of a warm, welcoming house. I know it can be a leap to think of cleaning the house as "family time," but you're doing it because your big-picture goal is to have a clean home. If it helps you to perceive chores this way, make house-cleaning time a true family activity—you can all clean together every Saturday morning for two hours while listening to energizing music.

Let's take the "Maximize Health" goal from the example in chapter 4 to illustrate further how scheduling activities works. Imagine this is your goal for the moment.

Major Life Category	Big-Picture Goal	Activities
Self	Maximize health	• Get enough sleep
		• Exercise 3 times a week
		• Eat home-cooked meals

To make sure you get to all the activities that support your goal, schedule on your Time Map enough sleep time to feel rested, block out exercise time three times a week, and schedule cooking time daily to prepare the healthful meals you want to eat.

TASK MASTERS

⏱ Time Map ⏱

ORGANIZING AND TIME MANAGEMENT PROFESSIONALS
(212) 544-8722

Time	Monday	Tuesday	Wednesday	Thursday	Friday	Saturday	Sunday
7:00 A.M.	Wake Up	Wake Up	Wake Up	Wake Up	Wake Up	Wake Up	Wake Up
7:00 –	PERSONAL – exercise	PERSONAL – sleep late	PERSONAL – exercise	PERSONAL – sleep late	PERSONAL – exercise		
7:30 A.M.							
7:30 –	PERSONAL – cook healthy breakfast, eat, get dressed						
8:30 A.M.							
8:30 –							
9:00 A.M.							
9:00 A.M.							
5:00 P.M.							
5:00 –							
5:30 P.M. –	PERSONAL – cook healthy dinner, eat, get dressed						
5:30 P.M. – 6:30 P.M.							
11:00 P.M.	Sleep	Sleep	Sleep	Sleep	Sleep	Sleep	Sleep

A TIME MAP BASED ON BIG-PICTURE GOALS

Now you need to fit these zones into your Time Map. Create a new Time Map that reflects your ideal balance.

Continue to do this for all your big-picture goals. Plot out your time for the whole week.

Now ask yourself, "Does my schedule have enough balance? Are *all* my major life categories represented? Have I made sure to include time for fun, rest, and play? Have I balanced physical and mental activities, social and private time? Does the pace seem right for my personality? Does the schedule I've set up energize me?"

Working out your Time Map is like working out a puzzle. Move things around. Try to make the pieces fit to your satisfaction. Of course, some things, such as your work hours or when a class is offered, can't be rearranged, but be as creative as you like scheduling everything else. If you're just starting out with this system, you may not be sure when the best time will be for you to grocery-shop (if you have access to a twenty-four-hour grocer, why not go ahead and zip through your shopping at midnight, when the store is empty?). Don't worry too much about it. If you don't know where to put something, always go with your first instincts. They're usually right—and if they're not, time will tell and you can adjust it later.

Once you've set up your Time Map, follow it for a couple of weeks. See how it feels. After you have seen it in action, you will be in a better position to evaluate it and make adjustments.

As you fill out your Time Map, there is a good chance you will run out of spaces to put things. If you have more activities than time, one option is to multitask, or layer, activities, which is explained below. In addition, you'll learn how to reduce your workload in chapter 8, "Purge."

Multitasking, or Layering

After you have created your Time Map, it may seem that you can't fit in all your activities. If so, think about whether you can multitask—that is, do two or more things at once.

Some activities, such as bill paying, proofreading, or driving, require so much focus that it's not feasible to layer another activity on top of them. However, many activities can easily be combined. You can schedule making phone calls to friends and family when you are cleaning your house (a cordless phone or headset makes this even easier). You can catch up on your reading or listen to books on tape when you are traveling by train or plane. You may even be able to do more than one thing at a time if the activities are no-brainers.

However, don't feel that you must always multitask or layer your activities. Sometimes it's nice to keep your time simple and focused. You are in charge of your time. If you get into the habit of always trying to squeeze in multiple activities at once, you may get a lot done, but you will feel frenetic and exhausted. Find the balance between multitasking and simple focused time that's right for you.

TIME MAPS IN ACTION

So, in what ways can your Time Map help you? It becomes the framework into which you place all the tasks that you do. It is your anchor and your compass in the storm of activity, demands, and opportunities swirling around you. It also gives you control, perspective, and a baseline for making decisions, as Miranda and Allie came to see.

Miranda's Time Map

Miranda was working without a Time Map, and it was severely hampering her productivity. She was a financial planner, and the two main facets of her job were to meet with clients and to design and manage their investment portfolios. She said it was important for her to accommodate her clients, so whenever a client called and requested an appointment, she'd say, "Okay, when would you like to meet?" and whatever time of day they requested, she'd say that would be fine for her. In her mind she knew she'd be planning to do portfolio work at that time, but she'd always give it up when a client asked for an appointment. The anxiety about the neglected portfolios would build and ultimately she'd end up staying at the office until midnight a couple of nights a week trying to catch up.

I suggested that she set aside a specific time for client meetings and a specific time for client project work each day. Since her clients usually requested morning or early-evening meetings, Miranda honored that preference by reserving every morning and two evenings a week for meetings. Then she reserved three hours each afternoon to design and manage her clients' portfolios.

Time	Monday	Tuesday	Wednesday	Thursday	Friday
9:30 A.M. to 1 P.M.	Meet with clients				
1 P.M. to 2 P.M.	Lunch				
2 P.M. to 5 P.M.	Design and manage portfolios				
5 P.M. to 7 P.M.		Meet with clients		Meet with clients	

MIRANDA'S WORK TIME MAP

Now, when a client requested a meeting, Miranda had a more proactive way of responding. Instead of asking an open-ended "When would you like to meet?" she'd ask, "Are mornings or early evenings better for you?" When all her morning and evening appointments were booked, she'd say, "Let's meet next week." If Miranda really wanted to accommodate a special client who needed an afternoon appointment, she could give up one of her financial planning sessions, but it would be a conscious decision. Then she'd work on portfolios one evening or morning to make up for it.

Using her new Time Map, Miranda went from crazed to calm in two weeks. That is truly the difference between someone who uses a Time Map and someone who doesn't.

Allie's Time Map

Allie, a mother with four school-age kids, was highly productive at work. She'd had a Time Map working for her at home, and she was doing relatively well managing her time until she reduced her work schedule from full-time to three days a week. She suddenly had Mondays and Fridays off—two whole days—but was surprised to discover that she wasn't getting to everything she planned to do.

In addition to wanting to have more time for relaxing, there were a million projects Allie wanted to get done during the day so that she could really focus on being with her kids in the evenings and on weekends. Now that she finally had the time to get the sofa reupholstered and read some novels, she found she wasn't getting to them. Instead, her days off were taken over by such mundane tasks as laundry and housework. Her informal approach to her two days off was not working. She needed a more formal plan.

Allie and I sat down and did a Time Map for her Mondays and Fridays. We decided she'd drive the kids to school, come home, and do *one* hour of meal prep, laundry, and house cleaning. On Mondays and Fridays, we set aside from nine A.M. to noon for home projects. Allie could plug any of her personal projects into these time slots.

From noon to three on Mondays, she'd run her errands. From noon to three on Friday, Allie would take some time for herself. She could have lunch with a friend, read a book, or go for a walk—it was *her* time. This Friday self time was her reward at the end of the week, and gave her something to look forward to.

Time	Monday	Tuesday	Wednesday	Thursday	Friday
7 A.M. to 9 A.M.	Drive kids to school, laundry, and housework				Drive kids to school, laundry, and housework
9 A.M. to 12 noon	Personal projects				Personal projects
12 noon to 3 P.M.	Errands time				Self time

ALLIE'S MONDAY AND FRIDAY TIME MAP

Without a Time Map, Allie's Mondays and Fridays had been free-for-alls. Whatever was urgent got her attention. Before she knew it the day was over, and she felt she hadn't gotten anything accomplished. When Allie created a Time Map and structured her days around her important goals, she was able to get to everything that was important to her.

MAKE YOUR TIME MAP WORK WITH YOUR PERSONAL STYLE

Your Time Map also offers a visual representation of what you have decided you want in your life; it reflects your unique values and choices. For example, the amount of structure you create within your Time Map will depend on your personal preferences. Even after you've set it up, you have flexibility in how closely you will follow your Time Map. If you thrive on structure, follow your Time Map to the letter. If you prefer more flexibility, you can be looser with it and give yourself the option to rearrange things occasionally. That's the beauty of a Time Map done properly: it's a truly customizable tool that you use in the way that works best for you.

A Time Map puts you in true control of *what* you do and *when* you do it. This even includes abandoning your Time Map when you need to. Part Three of this book will teach you the advanced techniques that will allow you to do this while still maintaining your ideal balance of activities.

Do Things at the Right Times for You

When scheduling activities, you need to consider your own personal energy cycles. What time is naturally best for you to do this activity? When do you *like* to do it? When do you do it best?

Jeremy was a busy book editor, whose goal was to read and edit manuscripts for a minimum of twenty hours a week. This work required a block of focused time. Jeremy's office was a madhouse of activity, interruptions, and ringing phones. Years earlier, he'd realized he needed to edit at home in order to get anything done. He'd go into the office in the morning, check the mail, meet with colleagues, and return phone calls. At noon, he'd go home and edit for the rest of the day in the privacy of his peaceful study.

Time	Monday	Tuesday	Wednesday	Thursday	Friday
9 A.M. to noon			Office		
1 P.M. to 2 P.M.			Lunch		
2 P.M. to 5 P.M.			Edit		

JEREMY'S OLD WORK TIME MAP

When he reviewed his Time Map and asked the question, "Does editing in the afternoons work for me?" he had to answer no. He was getting his editing done, which was his priority. But when he got into the office in the mornings, there would be a stack of urgent phone messages from the day before for him to return. Authors and colleagues felt they could never get hold of him. Also, he was often tired in the afternoons, which made the task drag on.

Time	Monday	Tuesday	Wednesday	Thursday	Friday
9 A.M. to 1 P.M.	Edit				
1 P.M. to 2 P.M.	Lunch				
2 P.M. to 5 P.M.	Office				

JEREMY'S NEW WORK TIME MAP

Jeremy realized that he'd had the right idea, but he was editing at the *wrong time*. He switched his editing time to the mornings. Then he'd spend the afternoons in the office, returning all the phone calls that had come in that morning. He'd get back to people the same day they called. His communication problems cleared right up. Jeremy just had to pay attention and make a simple adjustment for his Time Map to work beautifully.

Keep in mind that his Time Map represented his *ideal* schedule. On the days Jeremy had to attend morning marketing, acquisition, or production meetings in his office, he would come in, but he would make the necessary trade-offs to ensure he protected his twenty hours a week of editing time. Chapter 9 will teach you how to trade off tasks, while still maintaining your ideal balance.

Crisis Management

If you are a crisis manager, or if your energy levels are very erratic, you may not see how a Time Map could help you. It can, and here's how.

If you're what I call a crisis manager—someone whose job or life revolves around managing volatile or unpredictable factors—then your schedule can't be neatly designed around predetermined time zones. Maybe you're a mother with very young children, or a doctor, or a reporter. You're "on call."

Creating a Time Map for yourself is still possible. First, you've got to acknowledge that the core of your job is being available in a crisis. You have limited time for planned activities so when you create your Time Map, block out most of each day as crisis-management time.

Then make a list of the things that you consistently never have time for. Before you put anything on that list, ask yourself if it's really important, if it helps you achieve your big-picture goals. Let some things go and make compromises. When you're a crisis manager, you're not going to be able to get to everything. Do only what matters. You may have to give up serving on some committees, or lower your housework standards, or simplify your life in other ways. (Chapter 8, "Purge," will help you learn ways of streamlining your life.)

Take the list of tasks you decide you really want to do, and divide it into two categories: "*Must* dos" and "*Would like* to dos."

"MUST DO" TASKS. There is always someplace in your schedule for sacred, uninterruptible time in which to carry out your most

Time Map for Crisis Manager

Kerry—Sr. Partner of Law Firm

TASK MASTERS
ORGANIZING AND TIME MANAGEMENT PROFESSIONALS
(212) 544-8722

Time	Monday	Tuesday	Wednesday	Thursday	Friday	Saturday	Sunday
6:00 A.M.	Wake Up	Wake Up	Wake Up	Wake Up	Wake Up	Wake Up	Wake Up
6:00 - 7:00 A.M.	SELF—shower, dress, eat						
7:00 -	QUIET WORK (from home) — client matters						
9:00 A.M.	COMMUTE — reading briefs						
9:00 A.M. - 10:00 A.M.							
10:00 A.M.	OPEN — calls, questions, issues, e-mail						
1:00 P.M.	QUIET WORK — as needed from morning's open time						
1:00 - P.M. - 2:00 P.M.							
2:00 P.M.	OPEN — calls, questions, issues, e-mail						
6:00 P.M.	QUIET TIME — wrap up day, pack work for next meeting						
6:30 P.M.	COMMUTE — read law journal extracts						
7:00 P.M.							
	Sleep	Sleep	Sleep	Sleep	Sleep	Sleep	Sleep

important tasks. I've never met anyone who couldn't find some uninterruptible time to block off, whether it meant getting up a half-hour earlier, cutting a lunch break in half, or giving up a couple of weekend mornings each month.

I've also never met anyone who could truly be on call twenty-four hours a day, seven days a week without burning out. Not only do *you* suffer from no time off, but the people you're supposed to be serving also suffer from your burnout. Consider some renewal time a "must get to." Build it in.

Brendan was a high-powered physician who was constantly on the go. He had a flourishing practice, was on several committees at his hospital, and was very much in demand as a speaker throughout the country.

For Brendan, each day brought a new crisis. There were staff meetings, committee meetings, emergency care, and clinic duties. I asked Brendan to list the things that weren't getting done and were causing him serious problems. Preparing for presentations was number one on his list. He had to block time out for this. There was no way he could do it every week, but he was able to block out one Sunday evening a month. During that time, he was able to prepare his presentations for the entire upcoming month.

Another way to deal with "must get to" tasks is to squeeze them into every available moment you can find. This works if you have a lot of downtime—waiting time, traveling time, time spent on "hold," etc. Claudia was a salesperson who spent most of her time on the road making in-person sales calls to prospects. One of her "must do" tasks was to keep in frequent touch with her existing customers. Claudia's solution was to use her cell phone in every free moment to make calls. Between appointments, in her car, walking down the street, Claudia would call her customers, taking orders and resolving problems. She felt on top of things, and her customers felt they were receiving excellent service.

"WOULD LIKE TO DO" TASKS. What about tasks that you'd like to do, but that don't qualify as "must dos"? Lucy's kids were both under three years old. She wouldn't put organizing the pantry or doing yoga on her "must do" list, but she would love to get to these things.

For these tasks, we set up a "sudden opportunity" list, organized by how long each activity would take. When Lucy got an unexpected window of free time, she'd pick some tasks of the right length and do them. If, by some miracle, both her children fell asleep during nap time, Lucy would turn on the VCR and work out to a yoga tape.

When you're a crisis manager, your sudden opportunities can vary in length. You could find yourself with five free minutes or half an hour—or even a miraculous hour! You suddenly have time to yourself, but you spend half of the time figuring out what to do, and end up frittering away the opportunity.

Prepare yourself with a "sudden opportunity" list. This list should be divided into three categories of tasks. (If you've got a big project to do, break it up into smaller chunks before putting it on your list.)

- **Five minutes or less.** Make a quick phone call, read an article, back up some files on your computer, write someone a birthday card.
- **Thirty minutes or less.** Read a report, update your expense reports, cook dinner, clear out a file drawer, go for a walk.
- **One hour or less.** Search the Internet, work out, do a load of laundry, work on your business plan, pay your bills.

Anytime you think of something you need to do, ask yourself how much time you're going to need to do it. Then, when you get those sudden breaks, go to your five-minute, thirty-minute, or one-hour list and pick a task.

If you think you might get stuck with extra time before an appointment, or waiting in line, plan ahead and carry work with you. Bring a tote of magazines or professional journals and a highlighter, or bring that novel you've been dying to read. Just be sure that if these unexpected windows don't happen often, you still might need to schedule "catch up on reading" into your Time Map.

What If Your Energy Cycle Is Completely Unpredictable?

People who are suffering from depression or attention deficit disorder (ADD) or any other syndrome that prevents them from going full steam ahead have special Time Map challenges, too.

If you have an energy cycle that is unpredictable, stop beating yourself up. You need to think like a crisis manager. Accept what you're up against and build around it. Give yourself plenty of room.

Alexis, a self-employed travel agent who had ADD, needed

hours to get started in the mornings. Some days she couldn't concentrate on anything. Other days she would work like a maniac for twelve or fifteen hours straight. She couldn't predict how she would be able to function on any given day, so it was very hard for her to plan her time.

I worked with Alexis to pare down her to-do list to what was essential. We determined that out of the forty-hour workweek, she was usually highly functional for a total of only twenty-four hours. She never knew which hours these would be. Therefore, Alexis needed to plan only three days' worth of work for the week. That way, she'd be certain of getting to everything.

Gail's energy problem was temporary: she had recently gone through a bad breakup and was waking up every morning feeling lethargic. She decided the best way to work through this temporary state of depression was to swim in the mornings. This solitary, physical activity both relaxed and energized her for her day. She learned not to schedule anything social or anything that required mental challenges until the afternoons.

All of us go through periods where our energy fluctuates wildly for one reason or another. In chapter 11, "Equalize," you will learn how to adjust your Time Map to accommodate these situations. Your Time Map should always reflect your current interests, needs, and goals.

After you've developed your Time Map, you may be wondering the same things that my clients always wonder at this point: "Now I know that Saturday morning is my errand time. Which errands do I do?" "I've designated evenings as my family time. What am I supposed to be doing during that family time?"

This is where your to-do list comes in. Right now, all you are establishing is that cleaning time is Saturday morning. You are not determining that the toaster needs scrubbing! I'll discuss how to create and manage your to-do list in Part Three. Before we get to that stage, you need to select a planner in which you can keep track of your activities and tasks.

SUCCESSFUL TIME-MAP CHECKLIST

Adjust your Time Map until you can answer yes to all these questions.

- ☐   My Time Map reflects my big-picture goals.

- ☐   My Time Map includes time for all the categories I want to get to.

- ☐   I am able to concentrate on my chosen activity (during family time, I can concentrate on my family; during work time, I can focus on my work).

- ☐   I am doing my activities at the right times for me.

- ☐   My schedule makes me feel balanced and energized.

6

SELECTING A PLANNER
THAT WORKS FOR YOU

To keep track of the specific tasks that you are going to do within each activity zone, you need the right time-management tool. But there are so many choices: planners, organizers, calendars, palmtops, handhelds, PIMs, PDAs. How do you begin to choose what's right for you?

If you have tried using a planner in the past but abandoned it because it didn't work for you, chances are you made one of these three common mistakes:

1. You didn't pick a planner that was right for you.
2. You didn't take time to master its features and make it yours.
3. You didn't make it the one and only place to record your appointments and to-dos, so you never came to rely on it.

A good planner becomes an extension of who you are, so you have to pick the right one for you. To select a planner, start with an idea of the qualities you would like, go out and see what's on the market, and then bring one home and try out its features so that you can customize it for yourself.

No matter which planner you use, it's essential that you apply the "select one" rule: a single, consistent place where you record all your activities, appointments, and things to do. You have one life; you need one planner. When you have one planner on your computer, another in your bag, and a calendar on your refrigerator, it's cumbersome and confusing. Inevitably, as you transfer things from one place to the next, important things fall through the cracks. You need to rely on one planner to contain *all* your appointments and to-dos. While there is no perfect planner, you can find the one that's best for you.

The four main types of planners are:

- Wall or desk calendars
- Paper appointment books
- Computer programs
- Handheld electronic planners

To figure out which one you should use, start by looking at your natural preferences.

VISUAL/TACTILE VS. LINEAR/DIGITAL

Visual/Tactile

Visual/tactile people are most comfortable with a paper planner. Some clues that you are a visual/tactile person are:

- Your thinking flows most easily when writing things out, pen on paper.
- You remember things better when you write them down.
- You like to flip back and forth between pages in your planner in order to get events in perspective.
- You tend to remember where on a page you wrote things down. ("The phone number is on the lower right-hand corner of the page.")
- You write to-do lists in terms of association or groupings (things to buy, things to write, calls to make) rather than in terms of sequence, priority, and chronology.
- You enjoy storing your old notebooks to pore over years later.
- In general, you find computer technology cumbersome and time-consuming.

Linear/Digital

In contrast, if you are a linear/digital person, you would probably do very well with an electronic planner. Clues that you are linear/digital rather than visual/tactile are:

- Your thinking flows easily when you are typing.
- You are more likely to do a word search for a name or number than try to remember where you wrote a piece of information.
- You can look at one screen representing a day, or a week, and get events in perspective.
- You generally remember appointments by date, days of the month, times of the day. ("The concert is on Tuesday, two days after my husband's birthday on Sunday the twenty-sixth.")
- You think in terms of sequence, priority, and chronology rather than in terms of association or groupings.
- You don't feel the need to look back at what you've done in the past few days to plan out what to do today and later in the week; you mentally carry over your to-do list from day to day.
- You feel right at home with computers or electronics.

Visual/Tactile Options

If you are a visual/tactile person, you have two major options: wall or desk calendars and paper-based planners. Which one you choose will depend on how much information you have to deal with and how mobile you are.

WALL OR DESK CALENDARS. These calendars are useful tools for displaying the date and the day of the week. There are two circumstances in which a desk or a wall calendar could function as an important component of your time-management system.

1. If you work from one place all the time and your schedule is simple, you can use a stand-alone calendar to successfully

manage your time. One home-based business owner I know would record his appointments on his desk calendar. Each morning, he would check the calendar and write his to-do list on an index card, including any appointments he had that day. Then he would put the index card in his pocket and head out. Since his life was uncomplicated, this system was sufficient for his needs.

2. You can use your wall calendar as a communication device. This works well in families, where each family member can keep track of everyone else's schedule at a glance. Appoint one person to be the keeper of the calendar; he or she will confirm tomorrow's appointments with everyone at the end the day.

Wall calendars do, however, have two serious shortcomings as time-management systems. For one thing, they are not good for recording to-do lists. To-dos are interconnected with your calendar because for every task you need to do, you must ask yourself when to do it. Also, you can't exactly carry your wall calendar around in your briefcase. Therefore, you will still need a planner, and you'll get into trouble if you are recording appointments on both your desk calendar *and* in your planner. Select one; in most cases this will be your planner, because it's more convenient and efficient.

PAPER-BASED PLANNERS (AT-A-GLANCE, DAY-RUNNER, DAY-TIMER, TIME DESIGN FRANKLIN COVEY PLANNER, FILOFAX). These classic time-management tools work very well for many people even in this age of high-tech solutions. You don't have to spend a lot of time learning how to work with them, and recording information longhand in them feels natural. You don't need electricity or batteries. Moreover, if you think of a to-do item or need to schedule an appointment, you don't have to wait while you boot up or log on—you just jot down a quick note in your planner. Also, you can usually customize your system, using only the types of pages you need.

The downside is that if you lose your planner, you will be in big trouble. There is no easy way to back up your information. If other people need access to your calendar, it is hard to share it with them.

The biggest drawback is that if you have a lot of information to record, they can be quite bulky and heavy. For people who travel, this can be a big concern. Seeking streamlined versions of paper planners is the best alternative.

Linear/Digital Options

If you are a linear/digital person, you have two major options: computer programs and portable electronic planners.

If you decide to use your computer to manage your time, you will need to select software that has this capability, best known as a **personal information manager (PIM)** or a **contact manager**. Both of these applications have calendars, to-do lists, and address lists, but a PIM is really designed to manage yourself—your appointments or to-dos—whereas a contact manager is primarily a database program that helps you focus on everything you need to do for your clients; they work especially well for salespeople. For the purposes of the rest of this chapter, we'll be talking about PIMs because they have a broader application.

If you need something portable, one of the most powerful

options is a **personal digital assistant (PDA),** an electronic device. There are plenty of variations within PIMs and PDAs, and
they are not mutually exclusive—your PDA usually includes a
program for your computer that is compatible. This combination
does not technically violate the "select one" principle because
they work in tandem: you plug the PDA into your computer's
PIM, set them to synchronize, and immediately the computer calendar and PDA calendar update each other (and let you know if
there are any conflicting appointments).

**COMPUTER SOFTWARE (ACT!, OUTLOOK, DAY RUNNER, DAY-TIMER,
LOTUS ORGANIZER).** There are many computer software programs
that include a calendar with scheduling capability, a to-do list feature, contact management, and a place to store lists and notes.

If you are at your desk most of the day, you can get a lot out of
these programs. What's more, in a company setting, where many
people need access to your schedule, a network-enabled calendar is extremely efficient. Your assistant can update your schedule. Your colleagues can see at a glance when you are booked.
It's also easier to arrange meetings when everyone's agenda is
available on the network. You can input the names of the people
you would like to invite to your meeting and the program will
check prospective attendees' calendars, indicate any scheduling
conflicts, help you choose a better time if necessary, and send
out e-mail invitations.

Many free calendar programs are available on the Internet.
You can access your data with a password, and update your calendar on-line. If you give others access to your calendar, you can

inexpensively "network" your computer with theirs. Another benefit of these on-line services is that many of them will search the Web for information about concerts, films, TV shows, and sporting events you are interested in, and integrate the content into your calendar. A number of these "Internet-based calendars" are compatible with the major PDA and desktop calendar programs, so you can synchronize data.

While it's possible to use a PIM or contact manager on your desktop as your sole time-management tool, this requires you to print out pages and carry them with you. When you're out of the office, you have to record new appointments on paper, and enter them into the computer when you get back to your desk. This method can be cumbersome, so I don't recommend it. However, if you are disciplined enough to input this information as soon as you get back to your computer, or if you have an assistant who can enter this data for you, it might work for you.

You can use a computer-based calendar on your laptop, too, if you always carry your laptop with you, but it's inconvenient to boot up your computer and bring up the right screen just to check an appointment or to enter a to-do item. And unless your high-tech spouse and kids are all networked and plugged in, it's not a good planner for a family. Also, if your PIM isn't online, you must back up frequently to avoid losing all your information in a computer crash.

ELECTRONIC PLANNERS (PALM, SHARP, CASIO). These are lightweight and compact, and hold a lot of information. These products range from very basic, inexpensive electronic organizers to more costly personal digital assistants (PDAs) to pricey handheld PCs (HPCs), which are in effect miniature computers. In case the acronyms aren't confusing enough for you, there are powerful mini-computers also known as palm-size PCs (PPCs), PC companions (PCCs), or simply "palmtops." A basic PDA includes a calendar, a to-do list, a telephone and address directory, and a memo pad feature. The top-of-the-line palmtop can do almost everything your desktop computer can do, on a scaled-down basis.

One of the primary advantages of these electronic devices is that they are small and lightweight and can hold a lot of information. Also, they can save you inputting time: most electronic organizers and PDAs will allow you to input calendar data once, and view it in multiple formats—daily, weekly, and monthly—at the touch of a button. You can also program your electronic device easily to schedule recurring events: instead of writing "Monday morning sales meeting" every week in your paper planner for a total of fifty-two entries, you may enter the information once and hit a button, and your schedule will be updated for the rest of the year. Electronic organizers and PDAs also allow you to search for data by keyword or number.

The disadvantages to all electronic organizers are that using them takes more time than glancing at or writing an entry on a page of a paper planner. Also, it takes time to learn how to use PDAs, so many people who buy them end up using them simply as electronic address books.

PAPER-BASED PLANNERS

Pros	Cons
• There are no programs or systems to learn	• It can't do searches
• Writing feels natural and comforting	• It can be bulky
• It doesn't need batteries	• It's difficult to back up your information
• You can flip back and forth between pages for an overview	• Other people can't access your data
• You can store paper on the shelf for easy future reference	

DIGITAL PLANNERS

Pros	Cons
• You can perform searches for information	• You can view one screen at a time; it's hard to get a visual overview
• You can easily group and rearrange data	• The archive information is not as easy to use for reference
• It's easy to to back up your information	• Not as quick or instant as paper
• On a network, other people can access it	• Difficult for visual/tactile people to use

Going Linear/Digital When You're Visual/Tactile

Even if you're a visual/tactile person, you might choose to make the journey to an electronic/digital system if other people need easy access to your agenda. Or your company might require you to use a computer-based system. Or if you have a lot of information to record in your planner, the weight and bulk of a paper-based system might be too much for you. Finally, you might choose a PIM or PDA for security reasons, because these programs require a password to access your data.

If you're a visual/tactile person and you are going to try to use an electronic planner, you can train yourself to use a PIM or PDA, but keep in mind that it can take weeks or even months to feel comfortable with the system. In making the transfer, it is better to make the technology adapt to you, than the other fairground. Ask yourself what you like about your paper planner—how you use it, how you like to see your information—and then see if you can adapt your electronic program to work the way you think. If you have a choice of which planner to use, ask a lot of questions and do a lot of research, because you'll want to be sure that it will accommodate the way you organize information.

SIZE AND PORTABILITY

If you're mobile, you'll want to choose the smallest organizer that's feasible. If you are stationary, your time-management tool can take up as much space as you need.

Paper-based products vary in size, ranging from pocket-sized up to 8.5 by 11 inches. You need to consider two things: the size of your handwriting, and how much you have to write. If your schedule is packed and you have other people's schedules to keep track of as well as your own, you will need a larger planner. If you need a lot of space, but don't want to carry around too much bulk, get a planner with a smaller-ring circumference, and carry around only a month's worth of sheets at a time. If you are considering a computer program, check the available memory on your hard drive to be sure there's enough to run the program.

Electronic organizers are designed to be portable, and the competition to make the smallest and the lightest product is fierce. However, there is such a thing as too small. If you can't read the display without squinting, or if the screen is too small to accommodate your data, or the keyboard is too tiny to manipulate, you will not be able to enjoy your electronic organizer's other features, no matter how wonderful they are.

CALENDAR FORMAT

Whether you go with a paper-based or electronic planner, you need to consider which calendar format you'd prefer. Common paper-based planner formats are day-, week-, and month-at-a-glance. Your best bet is a planner that features both an overview of the month and a detailed view of either the day or the week, depending on how busy your schedule is.

In contrast, computer programs almost always provide multiple views, so you don't have to choose. You do, however, need to make sure the program allows you to input overlapping appointments.

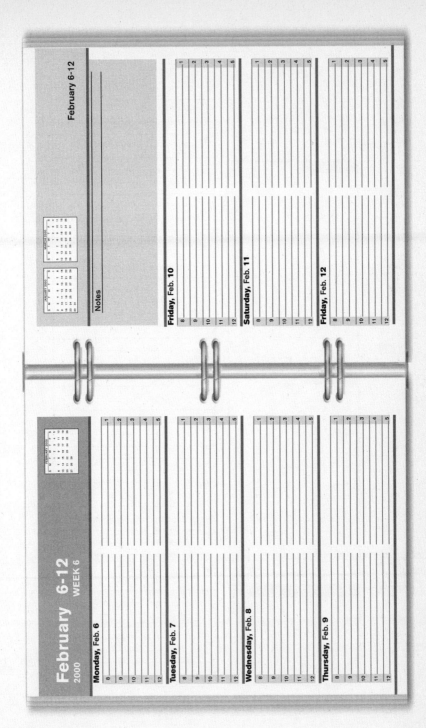

This week-in-view format works well when you have one to four items on your to-do list each day.

The one-page-per-day format is better when you have ten to twelve items on your to-do list each day.

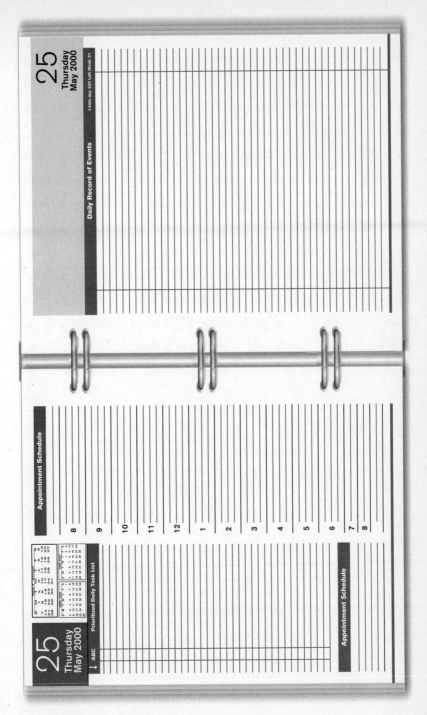

The two-page-per-day format works best when you have twelve or more items on your to-do list each day, plus you want to include additional information such as expense records, assistant's to-do list, etc.

For example, if you block out the time from two P.M. to five P.M. to work on a report, but you want to make a phone call at three P.M., will the program let you input that reminder? Some programs won't let you, and this can be a real limitation.

Another feature I recommend is that the program should visually indicate a block of time. For example, when you've recorded that two P.M.-to-five P.M. appointment, does the program clearly block off the whole three hours with color or a pattern? Or does the appointment show up only on the two P.M. line?

In addition to the calendar and the to-do list pages, all planners allow you to record and track everything from expenses to hours worked, books to buy, projects to do, phone numbers and addresses, birthdays, gift lists, and more. Select a planner that will allow you to record everything you would like to record.

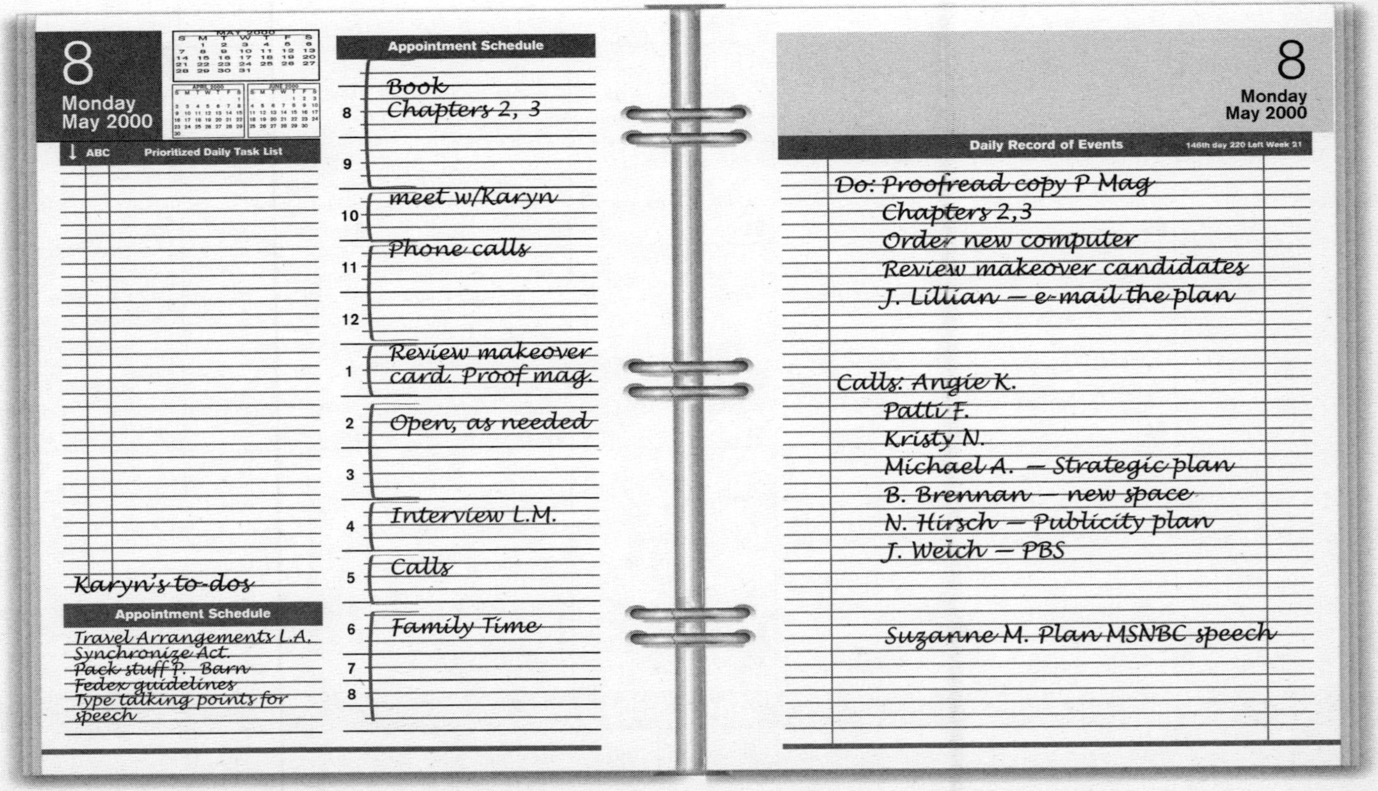
8
Monday
May 2000
ABC
Prioritized Daily Task List
Karyn's to-dos
Appointment Schedule
Travel Arrangements L.A.
Synchronize Act.
Pack stuff P. Barn
Fedex guidelines
Type talking points for speech
Appointment Schedule
8
Book
Chapters 2, 3
9
10
meet w/Karyn
11
Phone calls
12
1
Review makeover card. Proof mag.
2
Open, as needed
3
4
Interview L.M.
5
Calls
6
Family Time
7
8
8
Monday
May 2000
Daily Record of Events
Do: Proofread copy P Mag
Chapters 2,3
Order new computer
Review makeover candidates
J. Lillian — e-mail the plan
Calls: Angie K.
Patti F.
Kristy N.
Michael A. — Strategic plan
B. Brennan — new space
N. Hirsch — Publicity plan
J. Weich — PBS
Suzanne M. Plan MSNBC speech

Two-page-per-day paper format allows for visual groupings of types of tasks.

This month-view printout from a Palm Pilot allowed me to schedule the repeated task of writing from eight to twelve every day with just one entry.

May 2000

Monday	Tuesday	Wednesday	Thursday	Friday	Saturday	Sunday
1 9–1p Northwest #504–9:10AM–12:5... 4–5p Wendy P.–workingwoman	**2** 8–12p Writing TMIO 1–2p IMRA Handouts!!!	**3** 8–12p Writing TMIO 10–11p JFK to LAX	**4** 9–2p Writing TMIO 4–11p NAPO Convention	**5** 1–2p MSNBC–The Homepage 10–6p Rehearsal PBS special	**6** 8–12p Writing TMIO 4–11 NAPO Convention 10–6p Rehearsal PBS special	**7** 8–12p Writing TMIO 4–11p NAPO Convention 9–5p Taping PBS special 7p NW flight 1610 to Nashville
8 8–9a IMRA Set Up 10–11a IMRA Convention in Nashville 2–6p Writing TMIO 8–9p Fly back to LGA	**9** 8–12p Writing TMIO	**10** 8–12p Writing TMIO	**11** 8–12p Writing TMIO	**12** 8–12p Writing TMIO 1–2p MSNBC–The Home Page 5:15–6:30p Linda	**13** 8–12p Writing TMIO	**14** 8–12p Writing TMIO
15 8–12p Writing TMIO	**16** 8–12p Writing TMIO 10–4p Alex Linden	**17** 8–12p Writing TMIO	**18** 8–12p Writing TMIO	**19** 8–12p Writing TMIO 1–2p MSNBC–The Home Page	**20** 8–12p Writing TMIO	**21** 8–12p Writing TMIO

Monday	Tuesday	Wednesday	Thursday	Friday	Saturday	Sunday
22 8–12p Writing TMIO	**23** 8–12p Writing TMIO 10:15–11p Linda	**24** 8–12p Writing TMIO	**25** 8–12p Writing TMIO –6p Seminar Center	**26** 8–12p Writing TMIO 1–5p Do–eMail Terry regarding speech title Research statistics Sign books for IMRA folks Pay bills CALLS—*more*	**27** "... 8–12p Writing TMIO	**28** 8–12p Writing TMIO
29 8–12p Writing TMIO	**30** 8–12p Writing TMIO 10:15–11p Linda	**31** 8–12p Writing TMIO	**1**	**2**	**3**	**4**
5	**6**	**7**	**8**	**9**	**10**	**11**

CALL

❑ **MSNBC Woman-re: Segment**
Priority: 1
Due Date: 5/2/00

❑ **Kerry Rhodes–Jr. League Speaking engagement in Orange County**
Priority: 1
Due Date: 5/2/00

❑ **Carol M.–Hi there**
Priority: 1
Due Date: 5/2/00

❑ **Call Harry–Thanks**
Priority: 1
Due Date: 5/8/00
Note: Jm lm
Hl lm

❑ **Call "O" Magazine–Steven–Makeover Prospects**
Priority: 1
Due Date: 5/8/00

❑ **Call Lisa LaV.–re: application; CMA deposit slips. Jessi's deposits credited?**
Priority: 1
Due Date: 5/8/00

❑ **Call–Joe & Carol–Feedback?**
Priority: 1
Due Date: 5/8/00

DO

❑ **Merrill Lynch app**
Priority: 1
Due Date: 5/8/00

❑ **Thank You Note–Lilian**
Priority: 1
Due Date: 5/8/00

❑ **Thank You Notes–Oprah (+gift)**
Priority: 1
Due Date: 5/8/00

❑ **Challenges for Web Site**
Priority: 1
Due Date: 5/9/00

❑ **Thank You's–PBS folks**
Priority: 1
Due Date: 5/10/00

❑ **Title of NSA workshop to Terry**
Priority: 1
Due Date: 6/1/00

❑ **Thank You Notes–Journalists**
Priority: 1
Due Date: None

KARYN

❑ **Assemble statistics from TM survey**
Priority: 1
Due Date: 5/2/00

❑ **Pack stuff for Pottery Barn**
Priority: 1
Due Date: 5/8/00

❑ **Media Update–NSA, NAPO**
Priority: 1
Due Date: 5/8/00

❑ **Order cards from Levenger, plus other goodies**
Priority: 1
Due Date: None

❑ **Challenges**
Priority: 1
Due Date: None

❑ **OFIO Tech Chapter Update**
Priority: 1
Due Date: None

❑ **Check FFlyer miles applied to all recent flights**
Priority: 1
Due Date: None

❑ **Ainsley Harriot–airing?**
Priority: 1
Due Date: None

❑ **Thank Yous IMRA**
Priority: 1
Due Date: None

PERSONAL

❑ **Call Sue–re: trip dates**
Priority: 2
Due Date: 4/27/00

❑ **Eliz Irwin application**
Priority: 1
Due Date: 4/28/00

This is a to-do list printout from a Palm Pilot PDA. Notice how the tasks are sorted by category and priority. Due dates are listed, but the entries are incorporated with the calendar.

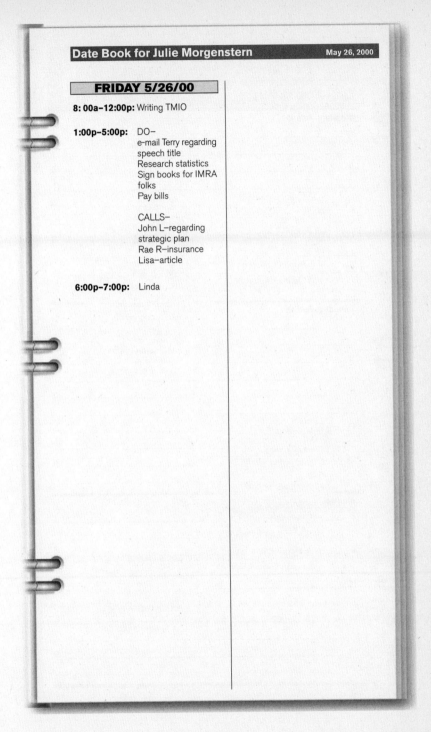

FRIDAY 5/26/00

8: 00a–12:00p: Writing TMIO

1:00p–5:00p: DO–
                    e-mail Terry regarding
                    speech title
                    Research statistics
                    Sign books for IMRA
                    folks
                    Pay bills

                    CALLS–
                    John L–regarding
                    strategic plan
                    Rae R–insurance
                    Lisa–article

6:00p–7:00p: Linda

You can integrate your to-do list with your appointments on a Palm Pilot by adding a note. The only drawback to this is that incomplete to-dos do not carry over to the next day.

February 2000

WEEK BEGINNING FEBRUARY 6

FEBRUARY 2000

S	M	T	W	T	F	S
		1	2	3	4	5
6	7	8	9	10	11	12
13	14	15	16	17	18	19
20	21	22	23	24	25	26
27	28	29				

Monday, Feb. 6

8 _____ 1

9 _____ 2

10 _____ 3

pick up supplies for barbecue

Discuss barbecue plans with Laura

11 _____ 4

30 min errand

12 _____ 5

20 min errand

20 min call

20 min errand

20 min call

20 min call

20 min call

Tuesday, Feb. 6

8 _____ 1

10 min call

9 _____ 2

10 min call

5 min call

10 _____ 3

11 _____ 4

Fill out application for kids' summer camp

12 _____ 5

20 min paperwork

15 min paperwork

Wedne

15 min paperwork

8 _____ 1

15 min paperwork

10 min paperwork

9 _____ 2

5 min paperwork

5 min paperwork

Fix drip in kitchen faucet

10 _____ 3

30 min fix it

11 _____ 4

15 min fix it

12 _____ 5

If you like to be more flexible with your to-do list, write your to-dos on small Post-It notes, cluster them, and move them around in your planner as desired.

BRAND

For paper planners, the brand is largely a matter of aesthetics. Go to a well-stocked office-supply store, and actually handle the organizers you are considering. Do you like the way the planner looks and feels? Also choose one with a presentation of time that makes sense to you and fits the way you work. Some work better if you are linear and think in terms of chronological lists; others are better suited for nonlinear thinkers who want to group notes by category on a page. If you are wavering, choose the one your first instincts tell you to choose.

For computer planners, consider whether the user interface presents time in such a way that you can easily work with it. Can you deal with having your to-do list on one screen and your appointment list on another? With software, you also need to consider whether the program is compatible with your hardware and operating system, and whether the company that sells it is likely to offer upgrades and support in the future. If you have an Internet connection, you may be able to download a trial version of the program you are considering, and spend a little time with it before you buy it. Try it out, and remember that while there is bound to be some learning curve, figuring out how to use an organizing program should not be so complex that you lose huge amounts of time feeling disoriented and nonproductive.

The big-name paper-based planners have corresponding software, so if you are making the transition from paper to electronic, look first at the brand that's already familiar and comfortable.

If you are buying an electronic organizer, consider how much memory it has and how easy it is to synchronize the information with your computer. In general, the very lowest priced models do not offer any PC connection, low- to mid-priced models use cables to transfer data to and from your PC, and higher-priced models use docking stations or infrared technology to make PC synchronization effortless.

You should also consider how you enter information into your electronic organizer. Lower-priced models offer small calculator-like pads, which can make data entry awkward. Higher-priced models, especially PDAs, come with touch-screen displays, stylus pens, or even keyboards.

If you want to use your PDA to send and receive e-mail, you will need one that comes with a modem and e-mail capability. (You will also need an Internet service provider [ISP] that works with your particular model.)

The technology keeps improving at a rapid pace and the price keeps coming down, so you have more choices than ever before, but there's no reason to buy a PDA that has whistles and bells you don't need. A simple electronic organizer will organize your time and to-do lists and addresses very well. On the other hand, if you are on the road or out in the field a lot, some advanced features like Map Quest on Restaurant Finder can be extremely useful.

YOU AND YOUR PLANNER

No matter which planner you choose, when you get it, you need to spend at least a week or two customizing it. Read the manual and then feel free to get creative from there. Decide where you are going to record different types of information (for example, appointments, addresses, to-do lists, expenses, etc.). Don't limit yourself to using it the way the planner company intended. You can ignore the times printed on the left, or write your journal in the section they allot to calls. If you have an electronic planner, you can usually alter the settings and options to suit your preference. Get familiar with the program's quirks and shortcuts.

Just be sure that you record in your planner *every* phone call, *every* project, *every* appointment, and *every* task on your to-do list, bar none. Don't make any exceptions. Plug in your annual events—birthdays, anniversaries, checkups, and car maintenance—at the beginning of the year. (If you are using a computerized system, you will be able to forward this information automatically into the next year.) Then create areas for any other information you'd like to record: family clothing sizes, room measurements, passwords, creative ideas, etc.

One trick you might use, if you like to be less structured about your to-do list, is to write your to-dos on small Post-It notes, jotting the time they will take and the types of tasks they are at the bottom of the notes. Overlap the Post-Its on the page, as shown on page 130. If you don't get to a task, you can pull off the note and stick it on a future page. If you do complete it, you can crumple up the Post-It note and throw it away. This tangible way of dealing with your to-do notes can be very gratifying.

Paper Management and Your Planner

One of the nicest things about your planner is that it's a fantastic paper-management tool. The piles of paper on most people's desks consist of things they are planning to do. You can easily live clutter-free if you file everything no matter what its stage of completion, and write in your planner what you need to do and when. If you have a mortgage application to fill out, first note in your planner what day you want to fill it out, then place the application in a "mortgage" file. When you get a meeting announcement, just record it in your planner and include all the pertinent information related to the meeting—the address, phone number, directions, and important agenda points. Then toss the paper.

This system will enable you to eliminate the paper reminders that accumulate on your desk, counter, bulletin board, and in your briefcase or handbag. Papers piled in stacks don't work well as reminders; they soon become visual Muzak, and you tune them out. Important papers get buried in the clutter. Your planner will save you from this fate.

The final thing to remember in your quest to find a planner that works for you is that none of them is absolutely perfect. You can find one that you love, adore, and come to depend on, but I have never met anyone whose planner didn't have a couple of irritating quirks. Pick a planner you really like, customize it to your heart's content, and then learn to live with its foibles. It will be a supportive, dependable friend for years to come, helping you achieve your goals and live your life to the fullest.

PART FOUR
ATTACK
Making It Happen

INTRODUCTION

Okay, so now you have a Time Map, a schedule that reflects your ideal balance and priorities. How do you actually make it work in the real world?

Your chosen activities (studying for your MBA, writing letters, spending time with your kids, cleaning your home) are still of a general nature. On a daily basis, you need to decide the specifics of each of those activities: i.e., *which* letters to write, *which* chapter to study, whether to read to your kids, play a game *or* go to the park; *which* room in the house to clean and how significantly. These specific choices are your daily tasks and to-dos.

Every day, you face myriad choices about your daily to-dos. There are things you want to do and things you have to do. In addition to your planned tasks, unexpected distractions come in every few minutes via mail, e-mail, telephone, and drop-by visitors. Unanticipated complications arise for each project you undertake, generating a whole new set of tasks and to-dos. Opportunities and temptations arise each time you read a magazine, surf the Internet, or attend a gathering. Not only are you bombarded by external interruptions, but you also have to contend with internal interruptions (sudden changes of thought, the impulse to procrastinate, the need to stretch or get a drink).

With all these demands on your time, how do you make good decisions about exactly what to do and when? How can you stick to the Time Map that you've so carefully planned out?

It's time to roll up your sleeves and begin the Attack stage, where you take your Time Map and your planner into the real world and make it happen. You will now figure out which tasks to let go, which to focus on, and how to get them done.

In *Organizing from the Inside Out*, I taught you how to use the SPACE Formula to untangle the piles of clutter in any room of your home or office. In part 3 of this book, I'm going to show you how to apply the SPACE Formula to untangle the chaos of to-dos that come your way.

The SPACE Formula for organizing your daily to-dos involves five steps:

- Sort potential tasks by category.
- Purge whatever tasks you can.
- Assign a Home to tasks you have decided to do.
- Containerize tasks to keep them within the time allotted.
- Equalize—refine, maintain, and adapt your schedule.

While this book devotes an entire chapter to explain each step of the formula, keep in mind that what I am really teaching is a very rapid thought process. Once mastered, Sort, Purge and Assign happen in an instant. Containerize lasts as long as each individual task you are doing, and Equalize becomes an ongoing part of your life.

In order for the SPACE Formula to work, it's essential always to have a copy of your Time Map visible and handy, either posted on a wall or on an index card in your wallet or purse. It will serve as a visual reminder of your schedule, priorities, and ideal balance. Together, the SPACE Formula and your Time Map will steadily guide you through the chaos, confusion, and crises you encounter as you manage your time. Now, let's get to it.

7

SORT

When your to-do list is crying out to you, it can be tempting to heed the call and quickly start in on it. But to manage your time well, you must use the SPACE Formula to handle your tasks. Start by sorting through your choices. For each item on your to-do list, ask yourself two questions:

1. Does this fit in with one of my chosen activities?
2. How long will this take me to do?

At this stage, you do not have to decide whether you will *actually do* the task or *when* you will do it. The sort phase consists simply of categorizing the task and estimating how long it will take to do.

QUESTION 1. DOES THIS TASK FIT IN WITH MY CHOSEN ACTIVITIES?

When faced with any task, ask yourself if it's part of an activity you have planned, such as learning more about investments or working out. If it is, you can consider doing it. If it isn't, remember that you carefully chose activities that will help you meet your big-picture goals. You will undermine your efforts if you take on extra tasks that aren't a part of your overall plan.

Let's say your neighbor asks you to volunteer to organize a fundraiser for your local park. If your big-picture goal is to serve the community, and you have designated a zone for community service in your Time Map, so you may consider doing this task. Remember, you are not *committing* to do the task at this point. You are only putting it through the first round of tests to see if it even warrants further consideration.

The object of the sort phase is to identify if and where an activity belongs in your schedule. Let's say you've set aside Saturday afternoons for family time. On Wednesday, when your son asks you, "Can you take me shopping for soccer cleats?" you know that on your Time Map, you have set aside time Saturday afternoons for this sort of activity. Or your friend Jeanie calls and wants to get together. You know that this activity goes in your friendship time on Monday nights, so you ask her if she wants to do something next Monday.

Every time you think of something you want to do, or are asked to do something, do this quick mental check—in which zone does this task belong? If it fits into a zone, it fits in with one or more of your big-picture goals.

Right now, don't worry about whether you will do the task or not. All you have to do at this stage is to figure out where the task fits in with your schedule, to begin to get a handle on how this task is going to affect other things you have planned.

If a task doesn't fit into one of your chosen activities, it likely doesn't serve one of your big-picture goals and so should not be done. Sometimes a task may help serve a goal but is not one of your chosen activities. Let's say your stockbroker suggests you attend a seminar to learn more about day trading. You have a big-picture goal of achieving financial security, and day trading might help that eventually, *but* your chosen financial activities for the next year are to clean up your debts and stay within a budget. At least for now, there's no room on your Time Map for learning about and monitoring stocks, so you decline the opportunity. Then someone offers you a freelance project that pays well. Since one of your chosen financial activities this year is to clean up your debts, and this extra income will help, you decide to consider this task. Now you'll have to consider how long it will take.

QUESTION 2. HOW LONG WILL THIS TAKE ME DO?

This is a question many people never stop to ask themselves. Or they might ask the question, but don't know how to accurately estimate how long things actually take. There are thirty-minute tasks and five-hour tasks, and if you can accurately calculate how long something will take, then you can realistically determine whether you can do it.

Try to be literal when making time estimates. So many of us have the verbal tic of always saying, "That'll take me two seconds," whether we're talking about getting dressed, making a call, or running to the store, and this affects the way we think about time. If you break this habit and start paying attention to how long it really takes to do things, you'll find yourself having a much easier time getting to everything you want to do.

Moreover, you should start asking others to specify how much of your time they need when they make requests. If your colleague says she wants to talk to you about a new procedure at work, find out if this will be a five-minute conversation or a half-hour one. People will respect you for setting boundaries for yourself, and may even become better at time estimating themselves—no more asking you, "Got a second?"

If you consistently miscalculate how long tasks take, you will find yourself constantly taking on more than you can handle, which will make your life very stressful. On the flip side, miscalculations may also cause you to avoid tasks.

For example, Beth's garbage disposal had been broken for eight months. She was sure all it needed was a fifteen-minute adjustment and was embarrassed that she had put off such a quick job for so long. We put the task through the sort process, and made the following calculation:

> ### HOW LONG WILL IT TAKE TO FIX THE GARBAGE DISPOSAL?
>
> 30 min.   Find the manual
>
> 15 min.   Read the manual
>
> 15 min.   Search toolbox for proper-size screw
>
> 30 min.   Shop at hardware store to buy proper screw
>
> 15 min.   Make adjustment to disposal
>
> 30 min.   Clean up
>
> **135 min.**   total
>
>
> 135 minutes divided by 60 minutes per hour = 2 hrs. 15 min.

It wasn't a fifteen-minute project, and somewhere deep down Beth knew it, even though she had never stopped to calculate! *That* was why she hadn't gotten around to it in eight months. She had to schedule more than two hours to get this job done.

When you've learned to estimate accurately, you will be less inclined to procrastinate. Once you know how long a task will take, even if it is a big project, it will seem more doable.

Estimating and Calculating

Calculating how long things take is not a mysterious talent. It is a skill anyone can master. It may take you two weeks to a month of practice to get the hang of it, but without a doubt, you *can* learn how. And it may be the most powerful time-management skill you tackle.

You might think that stopping to calculate how long tasks take is going overboard, but the truth is, this is one of the secrets of the best time managers. One Manhattanite I know has figured out that it takes her one minute to walk a block between streets and three minutes to walk a block between avenues, so she can quickly calculate to the minute how long it will take to walk from place to place. She's always on time, even when she doesn't wear a watch. Knowing that a simple calculation will keep her on schedule makes her feel confident and in control of her time.

Some people are resistant to calculating because they fear that if they examine honestly how long things take, they will realize they don't have enough time to do everything. My response is, Time management is a mathematical equation. If you ignore the truth in advance, you will only end up trapped in the reality, neglecting important tasks that you really wanted to get to. When you know what you're up against, you can plan and schedule accordingly.

Time Yourself

One way to learn the skill of calculating is to time yourself performing everyday tasks. Keep track in your planner as you go about your day. Note how long it takes to clean up after a meal, to write up your weekly report at work, or to read the newspaper. If you've never performed a task before, you can estimate based on how long it took you to do something similar. My brother Steve had ten weeks to study for his medical boards, an exam he'd never taken before. He knew from his years as a medical student that he could study effectively about ten pages per day. Using this as a baseline, he calculated and planned his study schedule.

STEVE'S STUDY SCHEDULE CALCULATIONS

420	pages of material
÷ 10	pages per day
———	
42	days of studying
÷ 6	days per week
———	
7	weeks

This calculation allowed him to see that it would take 7 weeks to get through all the material once. Then he would have 3 weeks to review or fortify weak areas. This put him at ease and gave him a schedule.

You won't always have to be this detailed in your estimates, but when you're up against a big, challenging to-do, it helps to have the ability to do such complex calculations.

The following exercise will help you become better at estimating how long things take. For the next week, as you create your to-do list in your planner, to the left of each task, estimate in writing how long you think it will take you to do. Your list might look like this:

Estimated Time	Task
(:10)	Make dinner reservations
(:15)	Write thank-you note
(1 hr.)	Create party invitation
(:30)	Pay bills
(:05)	Make doctor's appointment
(: 30)	Fix bicycle
(:15)	Back up computer
(:30)	Plan meeting at work
(3 hrs.)	Write speech

Then, when you do the task, time yourself, and write down the actual time it took to complete on the right. At the end of the day, your list might look like this:

Estimated Time	Task	Actual Time
(:10)	Make dinner reservations	:05
(:15)	Write thank-you note	:45
(1 hr.)	Create party invitation	3 hrs.
(:30)	Pay bills	Didn't do
(:05)	Make doctor's appointment	Didn't do
(:30)	Fix bicycle	1 hr.—still broken
(:15)	Back up computer	1 hr.
(:15)	Plan weekly meeting at work	(:30)
(3 hrs.)	Write speech	(2:15)

How accurate were your estimates? Most of my clients are shocked to see how much longer things take than they expected. Then again, occasionally they are surprised to see that a task they've been dreading because they thought it would be very time-consuming turned out to go far more quickly than they could have imagined.

It may feel unnatural and cumbersome to note the time estimate for each to-do item at first, but you won't have to be this detailed forever. Once you get some practice under your belt, you will remember how long certain tasks take. You'll develop an innate sense of how many calls you can fit into a morning, or how long it takes to pay the bills each week. After two weeks to a month of concerted effort, you won't have to estimate the time required for each and every five-minute task on your list.

However, even after you have become an excellent time estimator, come back to this tool when you are managing a large project, or during times of extreme stress, when you have to fit a tremendous amount into a tight time frame.

The more you practice, the better you will get at calculating how long things take. But be aware that there are factors that can throw off your estimates, most notably your inability to stay focused on one task at a time.

Starting and Stopping

People who constantly start and stop, interrupting their tasks and losing focus, often have an especially hard time estimating how long things take. Let's say at nine A.M. you sit down to prepare a presentation for an upcoming committee meeting. Over the next couple of hours, while working on the presentation, you receive five phone calls and make another ten, respond to twelve e-mails, and chat with three drop-in visitors. At four P.M., you finish the presentation but have no idea how long it actually took you to do it.

Some people are able to complete projects easily despite such interruptions because they can multitask (do more than one thing at a time) and shift gears quickly. For most people, however, working in this scattered way makes it difficult to get back on track, and productivity and work quality frequently suffer. On top of that, figuring out how long a project takes is difficult because one day you get a dozen interruptions and the next day you get three dozen.

If this is the case for you, you need to develop your tolerance for concentration. Start by blocking off specific amounts of time to do particular tasks and limiting your interruptions at that time. Put your phone on voice mail, ignore your e-mail and instant messages, and tell your visitors you will talk to them later. If you find yourself multitasking or constantly jumping up to make a phone call or stretch your legs, try your best to ignore it and stay focused for just fifteen minutes at a time. Do this several times a day for at least a week. Then try staying focused for thirty minutes at a time, then forty-five, and eventually stretch it to an hour, if you can.

This is a huge behavior change, and it will be challenging. Yet once you discover your true set-point for concentration (be it fifteen, thirty, forty-five, or sixty) your productivity will soar. You can break down all of your tasks into appropriate-sized pieces, and feel a sense of accomplishment you've never felt before.

The Hidden Time Costs

Another reason people incorrectly estimate how long tasks take is that they overlook hidden time costs. Emily was a novelist whose goal was to write for three hours every morning. So she'd schedule three hours of writing time. That was logical enough; however, she consistently got only two hours of work done each day. After paying attention to her habits, Emily realized it took her an hour to warm up. During this time, she read the newspaper, drank coffee, and gathered her thoughts. When she skipped this step, her writing was dreadful. She had to accept that part of her process included warming up. For Emily to write productively for three hours, she needed to schedule four hours. To calculate how long it would take her to write a piece, she would have to allow for this transition time.

When you are estimating how long a task will take, be sure to factor in more than just the exact amount of time it will take to do it. Here are some of the commonly overlooked time factors that can throw off your calculations.

TRAVEL TIME, TO AND FROM. People who don't calculate how long tasks take will walk into a building at ten A.M. for a ten A.M. appointment. Then they tap their toe waiting for the elevator, grit their teeth as it stops on every floor, step out and can't find the right door, and they swear that the world is conspiring against them. If this sounds like you, you can avoid these stressful scenarios by learning to take travel time into consideration. Will you be traveling at rush hour or driving past construction? Will you be using public transportation? How reliable is it? Is it an elevator building or a walk-up? Consider all the travel glitches that might slow you down and allow time for them.

SETUP TIME. Think back to Beth's garbage disposal. Actually fixing it was only a fifteen-minute task, but hunting down the materials—the manual that would explain how to do it, the right-size screw, the screwdriver—made the task much longer. When figuring out how long a task will take, factor in time needed for gathering materials or laying them out. Do you need to get yourself oriented to the project, or to read instructions first? Will you need to change your clothes (to work out, for example)?

FEEDBACK AND REVISING TIME. The very worst place to proofread a brochure is when you are standing at the counter at the photocopying store in front of the clerk, with a line of impatient people behind you. The pressure makes it very difficult to proofread accurately, but a lot of people find themselves in this situation because they don't factor in time for feedback and revising. Do you need to consult others before going forward? How long will it take to double-check your facts, edit, and polish? Do you have to wait for your boss to sign off on it before you can distribute it? Allow real time for these crucial steps and take the pressure off yourself.

STEWING TIME. Some tasks require thinking time. Like Emily the writer, you might need to gather your thoughts before you start, or you might need stewing time during the project. Leaving something you have written and coming back to it a day later can give you a fresh perspective. Difficult decisions, such as whether to make large purchases, can be more easily made when you take the time to stew. This contemplation time needs to be calculated into your schedule.

CLEANUP/WIND-DOWN TIME. Imagine yourself in the middle of a room, surrounded by hundreds of photos you pulled out because you were eager to organize them. Now it's time for you to move on to your next activity and it'll take at least a half hour to put them away so that you don't mix up the piles. The problem is you didn't factor in time for cleaning up, which is especially important when tackling a big project that can't be finished in one sitting. Even if cleanup time takes only a few minutes, if you've allowed yourself actual time for it you'll take a lot of pressure off yourself.

REFRESHMENT TIME. Often people are so eager to complete a project that they put their head down and work for several hours straight. But staying in one position or focusing on one thing for long periods of time can be grueling and in the long run may even make you less productive. It's important to take periodic breaks to move around or stretch or rest. Factor in time to do this, as well as for taking breaks for meals, snacks, drinks.

Calculating time for these hidden time costs can be very freeing. It's also helpful to recognize that sometimes an unexpected interruption or difficulty comes up and you fall behind. The solution to this is building cushions of time into your schedule. Even if you're certain that shoveling your driveway will take fifteen minutes, allow a few extra minutes just in case it takes longer than you thought—maybe the snow is heavier than usual. That extra time cushion will keep you from being late to work. And if you'll be doing the task at a time of day when you're very likely to be interrupted, or if you've got kids around, build in an even larger cushion so that an interruption or two don't throw your entire schedule off. When in doubt about how much cushion time you'll need, factor in an additional 20 percent.

Once you learn to ask yourself how long each task will take—and make realistic estimates—you'll see that you do have too much to do. This is good news! It will inspire you to develop other time-management skills that will help you reduce your workload, such as creating shortcuts for routine tasks, delegating, and mastering the diplomatic art of saying no. You are now on your way to becoming a better time manager!

Calculating How Long Unfamiliar Tasks Will Take

If you've never performed a particular task before, especially if it is a complicated one, it can be very helpful to ask someone else who has done it before how long it took. Sometimes it's helpful to ask several different people, keeping in mind that it takes different people different amounts of time to do the same task. This will give you a rough idea of what to expect. For example, let's say you have to move your entire family across the country, and you haven't packed up and moved since you were in college and had only enough possessions to fill a dorm room. Others who have moved a houseful of items can clue you in to not only how long the whole process took, but how long each element of the task took: gathering packing materials, packing, conducting a garage sale and/or donating items, cleaning up the house afterward, transferring mail and phone service, etc. Getting an accurate idea of how long the whole process will take, and how long the various parts will take, will probably inspire you to take the next step, purging, in which you will delete, streamline, and delegate tasks.

Indeed, the sorting process and the calculations you do make it so much less intimidating to face a long list of to-dos and will encourage you to move forward. So sort through your current list of to-dos and then you can continue through the SPACE process.

But wait—what about that huge backlog of to-dos that has been piled on your desk or kitchen table for months? My advice is to ignore it until you've put your current list of tasks through the SPACE process. For one thing, dealing with your current to-dos may make it clear that some of those old ones can be crossed off your list. For another thing, it's just too much to tackle all your tasks at once. However, when you're ready, here's how you will tackle that intimidating backlog.

SORTING IN ACTION: TACKLING A PILE OF TO-DOS

After you've developed the skill of calculating how long tasks take, and you've gotten used to thinking about tasks in terms of what activities and zones they can be a part of, it will be much easier to deal with a backlog of to-dos. Here are some general tips.

- Set aside a minimum of two hours per session to go through the backlog.
- Avoid using this as a catch-up session. Don't stop to actually "do" any of the to-dos. Simply sort to see what you have.
- Start with the most recent pile, the center of the storm, to get a grip on what's most relevant and current.

Here's an example of how to sort through a backlog of tasks. Fiona was a mother of four who worked full-time—her schedule was *packed*. The desk where she performed her household tasks was piled high with papers that needed attention. There was not one moment when she didn't feel stressed, with this huge pile weighing on her mind.

We started by going through the stacks item by item, sorting. What was in there? Warranty cards, receipts for items that had to be returned, gifts and cards to be sent, reminders to call about household repairs, insurance forms, bills to pay, requests for donations. As we looked at each piece of paper, she jotted down on a Post-It note her estimate of how long it would take to do that task and posted it on the paper.

When we'd gone through everything on the desk, we added up how much time the pile represented. It turned out to be nine and a half hours' worth of to-dos. Fiona was shocked. Like most people, she believed that if she could just get three uninterrupted hours at her desk, she'd get all caught up. What an underestimation!

Fiona had feared her backlog of to-dos for years. Although quantifying it was overwhelming to Fiona at first, this story has an even happier ending. The sort process is only the first step of the SPACE Formula. In the second step, purge, we went on to reduce those nine and a half hours to three!

Fiona was thrilled. There was no way she would have reduced her burden without honestly looking at what it was. When she honored the reality instead of denying it, that was half the battle. For the first time, she was in a position to do something about it.

At the end of the sort phase, you know that the tasks on your list all fit in with your selected activities and support your big-picture goals. You also know where they belong on your Time Map, and how long they will take you to do.

However, that doesn't mean you have committed to actually *doing* all these tasks. You are taking a proactive approach to all the options and demands life has thrown at you, and you are facing your situation head-on. You may still have too much to do, but now you are in a powerful position to do something about it. That's what the next step, purge, is all about.

8

PURGE

By this point, you have sorted your tasks by chosen activity, and you have estimated how long they will take. If you are like most people, you've probably discovered you still have much more to do than you can possibly accomplish. Your next step is to reduce your workload—and your stress level—by getting rid of certain tasks, or "purging" them. After all, just as you can fit only so much into a closet or drawer, you can fit only so much into your waking hours.

Your Time Map will instantly highlight the fact that if you expand the time for one activity zone, you will have to reduce the time for another. For example, as you look at your Time Map, you see you have designated three hours to do errands on Saturday. Yet when you add up your errands for this week, you realize it will take you four hours to do them. You could choose to do all four hours' worth of errands, but this choice means cutting into that hour of your afternoon you've allotted for an outing with your child.

When you have more tasks than time, you have three options:

1. Delete tasks.
2. Create shortcuts to do tasks more quickly.
3. Delegate tasks.

DELETE TASKS

Often, you will need to delete tasks from your list simply to keep the balance in your life. Certainly any working parent would agree that he or she is juggling several full-time jobs—raising kids, building a career, managing a household—any one of which could monopolize all the available time. If you have many roles and responsibilities, you will inevitably have far more potential tasks in each category of your life than you could possibly carry out.

When having to decide what to toss, ask yourself which tasks are the most important, which choices will help you accomplish your goal most effectively and efficiently. Then, too, ask yourself whether any of the tasks you are considering will help you accomplish more than one goal. The more goals a given task will help you accomplish, the greater its value to you.

Let's say you've set aside three hours every Monday afternoon to make sales calls. You've generated a list of thirty prospects and know you can call only about twenty in a three-hour period. You decide to let go of the ten cold calls and just phone the hot prospects.

Or perhaps you have designated Sundays for family outings. Your family comes up with three different ideas for the upcoming Sunday: seeing a movie, having a picnic, or going for a bike ride in the park. Since another one of your goals is to get in shape, biking is the winner for this week, and you eliminate the other two ideas.

The Art of Saying No

More often than not, the act of eliminating tasks involves saying no to other people. If it's hard for you to say no, you will end up doing things you don't really want to, simply because you feel guilty declining. We all hate to disappoint, but the fact is, other people will *always* ask you to do things for them. You have to learn how to balance doing things for those you care about while still honoring your own goals.

To do this, you must recognize your right to say no. Only *you* have your eye on your big picture. Only you can decide what fits into your Time Map and what doesn't. When you say no to someone's request for your time, you can be polite and considerate; saying no does not mean you have to be abrupt or rude. When saying no, you're not obligated to go on at length about why you are saying no. You may choose to at times, particularly if you are talking to someone with whom you have a close relationship, but don't feel you have to.

Two, you need to get good at saying no. If you're not used to it, prepare some answers in advance and memorize them. That way you won't be caught off guard and find the words "Yes, of course I will" popping out of your mouth. You know the types of requests you are likely to encounter, and can compose some tailor-made answers that suit your situation. Here are some ideas to get you started.

- **To decline an invitation to an event you can't attend.** "Thank you for thinking of me. I'd love to attend, but unfortunately, I can't make it."
- **To a telephone solicitor asking you to make a contribution.** "I plan my charitable donations at the beginning of the year, and I never vary from it. Please remove my name from your list."
- **To the head of the PTA.** "That sounds like a great project, and I'm flattered you think I am the best person to handle it, but I'm too busy to do justice to the project right now."
- **To someone who keeps insisting.** Don't explain further or you can be outmaneuvered as the other person finds yet more reasons why you should be able to accommodate the request. Just smile and keep repeating, "I'm sorry, I can't," "No, thank you," and the good, old standard: "No."

Practice saying "I'm sorry, I just can't" and "No" out loud. Say them with firmness and conviction until they feel natural.

But what if the person making requests is your boss? It may seem impossible to say no in that case, yet I promise that sometimes you can. If your boss keeps piling "urgent" projects on top of you, creating an unrealistic workload, ask his or her help in prioritizing the tasks. Present the situation in a calm, nonjudgmental manner, and suggest how the problem might be resolved: "I know you want me to do the computer project, which will take five hours, and I'd be happy to write your speech for the conference, which will take me about six hours. The challenge is, I can't do both before the end of the day. Which is more important to you? Or can we find someone else to take on at least a piece of one of these projects? Or can we wait a day on one of these projects?"

Then, honor your boss's decision. (This approach is also effective with clients who keep piling work on beyond the original scope of the project and kids who have a hard time hearing no.) The key is making other people aware of how long it will take to do what they are requesting. Inadvertently, you're teaching them the skill of calculating tasks, too!

STREAMLINING ROUTINE TASKS

Instead of eliminating tasks completely, another option is to create shortcuts and streamline to get the job done in less time. If you're like a lot of people, you feel your life is eaten up by drudgery. When you spend too much time on tedious, repetitive details, you are left with less time for other activities that help you achieve your big-picture goals. By investing a few hours creating streamlining systems for routine tasks, you can eliminate a lot of grunt work.

There are many ways to streamline. Sometimes you can skip certain steps in a job to make it go faster. You can create master lists and forms to take the thinking out of repetitive tasks. Designing simple routines will reduce decision making so that you can do things more quickly. When you have to think, remember, weigh your options, and agonize over every small task, it takes a lot of time, not to mention mental energy. But when you make decisions in advance, you free up time to focus on and be ready for activities that are more meaningful to you.

Of course, sometimes we reinvent the way we do things because it feels creative. But if you find yourself rearranging the spice rack or reformatting your company's newsletter for the third month in a row, ask yourself whether you couldn't spend your wonderful creative energy on far more interesting and productive activities.

So spend a few minutes redesigning how you do things. It can pay off in hours saved in the long run.

What to Routinize

To minimize drudgery, I urge you to evaluate almost all tasks that you do on a repetitive, routine basis to see if you can dream up ways to do them faster. Housework and routine office chores are prime candidates. The Americans' Use of Time Project at the University of Maryland revealed that the average American spends more than twenty hours a week on housework. According to Declan Tracy in *Clear Your Desk,* the average office worker spends over twelve hours a week on routine handling of mail, filing, and searching for things.

If you identify your regular chores and break them down into their consistent elements, you'll probably get some ideas about how to streamline them. Think about how to eliminate the hidden time costs of travel, gathering materials, revising, and cleanup and you'll probably come up with many clever ways to keep the drudgery from eating up all your time. Here are some shortcuts to get you started.

Routines and Checklists for the Home

• **Post a "Remember to Take" checklist** by your front door and review it before leaving the house, e.g., "Remember to take your wallet, keys, planner, checkbook, umbrella, kids' backpacks, homework, ballet shoes, soccer equipment, cell phone, and charger." Laminate the list if you like and hang it on the inside of your coat closet.

• **To simplify grocery shopping, meal planning, preparation,** come up with two or three weeks' worth of meals (keeping in mind taste, ease of preparation, and cleanup), then rotate them. Designate Monday as taco day, Tuesday as grilled chicken and potatoes day, etc. If you love to cook, use weekends for your more creative meals.

• **Create a master shopping list.** Put your standard groceries, including brands and sizes, on it. To save even more time, organize your shopping list according to your grocery store's layout. Type up the list, make several copies, and post it on your refrigerator. As you run out of items, check off what you need. When it's time to go shopping, you can simply grab the list and go. This can work at the office, too, for office supplies.

• **Set up your laundry space so that it includes all the items you need to do laundry.** Include a table for folding clothes and a rod and empty hangers so you can avoid ironing by hanging clothes as soon as they come out of the dryer. Assign a basket for each family member; each person can come and take his or her own stuff and be responsible for putting it away.

• **Simplify the color scheme of all your clothes.** Learn which colors look great on you, and shop from within that color family. Working within a color scheme reduces the time you spend thinking, searching, and making decisions about what to wear or what accessories will match your outfits. Also, if you always buy the same style and color of socks, you'll save a lot of time matching up pairs.

• **Come up with a favorite wedding gift and baby gift, and designate these as the gifts you will give every time.** For example, whenever you are invited to a baby shower, you might always give a beautiful baby blanket or a basket of baby books. This saves a lot of decision-making time. If this feels too limiting to you, pick one store that you always go to when you need to buy a baby or wedding gift.

• **Buy all your greeting cards for the year ahead at one time.** Don't waste time searching for the perfect card every time a birthday or anniversary approaches. Once a year, buy all your cards, fill them out, address them, stamp them, and write the date each should be mailed on the spot where the stamp goes. Store them by the front door or with your bills to pay, then stamp and mail them out on the date designated on the envelope. Or skip the snail mail card altogether and bookmark a site that sends virtual birthday cards, and have the electronic greeting sent out in five minutes' time.

• **Subscribe to an on-line special-event reminder service.** You send the service a list of the events you want to remember, and ten days before the special day, they e-mail you a reminder along with some gift suggestions. You can order the gift on-line and have it sent directly to the recipient. On AOL, go to "My AOL" and select "Reminder Service" to find out more.

• **Set up a bill-paying center in your home wherever you like to pay the bills.** Stock that center with everything you need for the job—checks, envelopes, stamps, pens, and a calculator so you don't have to search for them every time. Keep your receipts and bill-paying records in portable file boxes nearby to prevent a backlog of filing.

• **Set up automatic payments for bills you pay every month.** You can set up automatic payments for insurance payments and the like. If you do your banking on-line, you can also set up payments for utilities and other monthly bills, then go in once a month, indicate how much you want to pay, and the computer will transfer the money from your account to the payee's. Check with your bank to see if they provide this service.

• **Establish a set daily clutter pickup time.** Do it right before bed, right before dinner, or first thing in the morning. When you have a set time, you're not distracted the whole day thinking, "I really should do the dishes," and you can stick to your chosen tasks.

• **Set regular days for house cleaning.** You might decide that every Wednesday you'll clean the bathroom, every Friday you'll clean the kitchen. When you clean just one room at a time you don't waste time running from one room to the next.

• **Learn how to clean efficiently.** Jeff Campbell's book *Speed Cleaning* explains how a three-person cleaning team can go through an average house in forty-two minutes. For example, he suggests that you move from high to low, letting the dust from the top shelves fall on the floor, where you can vacuum it up.

- **If you can afford it, hire someone to do the deep cleaning.** That way you just have to schedule time for daily pickups.
- **Declutter your home.** Cleaning professionals say eliminating clutter can reduce housework by as much as 40 percent.
- **Make a master travel checklist.** Include on the list categories of clothing, plane or train tickets, passports, camera, medicines, toiletries, etc. You can customize quantities and garment weight according to the length and climate of each trip.
- **Keep a toiletries bag pre-packed with duplicate soap, toothpaste, toothbrushes, etc.** There's no need to waste time gathering and packing these items every time you go out of town.
- **Before leaving on a trip, print out or write up address labels for those to whom you will send postcards.**
- **Make a reminder list of last-minute things to check as you're leaving the house for a trip**—have you watered the plants, turned on the alarm system, and unplugged any extra appliances?
- **Create computer templates for all the documents you find yourself typing over and over.** Feel free to modify the ones that come with your word processing program or design new ones. The procedure may vary slightly from one program to the next, but usually you just create a new document, design your form, then save it as a template instead of a document.
- **Create form-letter templates.** While you don't want your correspondence to sound like form letters, writing every letter from scratch is an enormous waste of time. Create templates for

pitch letters, proposals, thank-you notes, overdue bill notices, and any other type of document you write regularly.

- **Keep your filing system simple.** If your files are complicated you will find yourself procrastinating because it takes so long to figure out where to file a document. Experiment with color-coding files so that you can instantly see what type of file it is (such as green for financial files, purple for personnel). The key to keeping up on your filing is to make filing easy and convenient, so be sure too to place your file cabinet within arm's reach of your desk chair. If you have no room for a traditional filing cabinet, use portable file boxes or a file cart on wheels.

- **Use forwarding Post-It notes.** If you use a paper planner and do certain tasks on the same day every week (let's say you pay your bills every Friday), write the task on a Post-It note, stick it on Friday's page, and at the end of the day move it to the page for next Friday. Personal digital assistants such as a Palm Pilot allow you to do this electronically through a feature called "repeat task" (see page 115 for more on PDAs and to-do lists).

STREAMLINING NONROUTINE TASKS

Even when your task is one that you don't do on a regular basis, you can still find ways to streamline it. One way to do this is to skip steps. Getting back to our example of moving across the country, you may feel that you ought to have a garage sale to get rid of your excess clutter that you don't want to move. However, if it will take you five days to price everything, put it in the garage, advertise, and run the sale, maybe it's not worth the extra money you'll make given how much time you will have to block out for this project. Maybe your primary goal is to move, not to make every dime you possibly can. Give yourself permission to let the tag sale go. Similarly, if your company is launching a new service and you have one month to hire people to provide that service, train them, create a brochure, and do a mailing and a launch party, ask yourself if all these steps are absolutely necessary. Maybe you can shortcut the step of developing a brochure and instead print a simple postcard that says "come to our launch party and find out about our great new service."

Then, of course, you can create shortcuts for yourself by delegating jobs. Hire movers to pack, or hire caterers to prepare and serve refreshments at the launch party. Delegate the part of the job that is the most unfamiliar to you. You won't always want to spend time learning a new skill to get the project done. Let someone else figure out how to keep the appetizers warm on the way from point A to point B.

Another way to streamline is to lower your standards: you don't always have to do "A" quality work. Consider how important the task is; do you have to have a perfectly polished report if it's just an in-house document for your colleagues, or do you have to impress your boss?

DELEGATE TASKS

If you have determined that a task absolutely must be carried out, and you've streamlined it so that it will take the least amount of time possible, the next step in purging it from your schedule is to consider delegating it to someone else.

When you authorize others to take over some of your activities, you free yourself to focus your time and efforts on those tasks where you can make your best contribution. (Be sure you haven't skipped over the eliminating and streamlining steps, however. You certainly don't want to eat up extra time by having your helper do more than is necessary to get the job done—and if you're paying her, it's all the more reason to streamline the job beforehand.)

One of the overlooked and yet most delightful aspects of delegating is that it allows for a very healthy interdependence among people. When you work as a team, it brings people together. Relationships solidify as you share the workload and learn to rely on one another.

Effective delegation is one of the most important time-management skills to master and employ, yet there are many reasons that people have trouble redistributing some of their workload to others. Here are some of the most common ones.

• **You feel too busy to delegate.** When you are overwhelmed with things to do, it can feel like you don't have the time to invest in delegating and supervising someone else. However, investing a few hours or even minutes figuring out what you can delegate, finding someone to help, and training him or her can save you enormous amounts of time. Don't be afraid to take time out to formulate a plan.

• **You feel guilty "dumping" on others.** If you think of delegation as giving someone else the undesirable or grunt work, you may feel guilty about doing it. After all, none of us wants to be the big bad boss. Then again, you don't have to martyr yourself to prove that you don't think you are above certain tasks. Remember, just because you don't like doing a task doesn't mean someone else won't enjoy it. We all have different skills, interests, and talents, so don't feel guilty asking someone else to help. Delegation works best when you put the right person in the right job at the right time, and allow everyone to make an important contribution to the success of a goal.

• **You have difficulty depending on others.** Some people are imprisoned by an "If I don't do this myself, it won't get done right" mentality. If you grew up in an environment where you couldn't depend on the adults around you, it will be especially hard for you to depend on others.

Think of delegating an opportunity for personal growth. It will give you a chance to break past your childhood experience where you may have been the only person who *could* do things right, and discover that other people can offer fresh and wonderful ideas. Focus on the fact that like you, most people are responsible and intelligent, and like to make a contribution.

• **You're afraid of becoming dispensable.** You may resist delegating because you are afraid that if someone else can do your job, you will no longer be needed or have value. If you really thought about it, you would probably see that other people's need for you is not tied up in just one task or your ability to handle several tasks at once. You have a reserve of unique skills, ideas, and personal traits that make you valuable to others. So let go of tasks that other people can do and free yourself for new projects.

What to Delegate

There are two categories of tasks that can be delegated most easily:

- Noncreative, repetitive tasks done on a regular basis (washing dishes, bookkeeping, faxing, assembling packets, interviewing perspective employees).
- Special projects, onetime or infrequently done jobs (creating a brochure, planning a trip, buying a new computer).

This distinction will help you when you are determining whether the task is worth the effort of delegating. For routine tasks, it is almost always worth investing time to train someone else. An initial investment of time will free you up for years to come. For special projects, consider the scope of the undertaking. If it would take you longer to train someone than it would to do the project yourself, and the project won't have to be done in the future, it is more efficient to do it yourself.

You should also consider delegating the following kinds of jobs:

- Tasks you aren't good at doing, and that someone else can do better.
- Tasks you don't enjoy
- Tasks that deplete you of energy or time you need for more important activities.

One of the reasons it can be hard to delegate is because we forget that delegating is not just about doing what you like and getting rid of the tasks you hate. Good managers delegate assignments they enjoy doing when they have higher-priority tasks to do, or if someone else could do the job more efficiently. In addition, sometimes you are truly the best person on the team to do a task you dislike.

Determining Which Jobs You Will Do

After you have evaluated the jobs and the steps, decide what you will do yourself and what you will entrust to others. As you scan the components of each job, ask yourself where your time is best spent and where you can make the greatest contribution. Consider your talents, vision, skills, and preferences. What can only you do, or what can you do to best serve your goals?

Reserve those tasks for yourself and delegate the rest. Sometimes, it makes the most sense to delegate the entire job and serve simply as the supervisor. In the case of big, expansive projects, if you get too involved in the details, you will lose sight of the big picture and not be able to lead as effectively.

Delegation Planning Sheet

To determine specifically what to delegate, it's helpful to write out a plan for delegating. Take a piece of paper and divide it into four columns. In the first column, put the big-picture goal. In the second column, list all the specific activities involved in accomplishing the goal. In the third column, estimate the time that each task will take. In the fourth column, indicate who you think is best suited to the job, considering such factors as what it takes to get the job done and the availability and reliability of the person.

Big-Picture Goal	Specific Activities	Time Required	Best Suited
Have a clean, comfortable, welcoming home	• Daily pickup	15 min./day	Dad?
	• Take out trash	5 min./day	Jim?
	• Weekly deep cleaning	8 hrs./week	The family? Or a housekeeper?
	• Weekly food shopping	1.5 hrs./week	Mom?
	• Home decorating	2 hrs./week until done	Mom?
	• Gardening	2 hrs./week, spring and summer	Dad?
Become substantial business in this region by offering outstanding customer service	• Respond to calls with a human voice	24 hrs./day	Team of receptionists? Or voicemail between midnight and 9 A.M.?
	• Monthly "tips" mailings	12 hrs./ month	Outsource to newsletter company?

Big-Picture Goal	Specific Activities	Time Required	Best Suited
	• Send out birthday cards to clients	$^1/_4$ hr./day	Reception-ists?
	• Follow-up call to every service visit	1 hr./day per salesperson	Sales-people?
	• Free monthly seminars	12 hrs./month	Company president?

Review your list and double-check that you have not included unnecessary tasks on your list of things to do. If a task doesn't need to be done, don't delegate it—just eliminate it.

Who Is the Best Person for the Job?

As you're deciding on whom to delegate to, keep in mind that there are three kinds of delegatees, each requiring a different investment of your time.

1. **Delegate to an expert.** Give the job to someone who can do it better, faster, or more efficiently than you. This requires the least investment of time on your part and provides an almost instant time savings. For example, hire a lawyer to take care of the collections problem. Hire a handyman to hang the bookshelves, as his or her knowledge of how to find studs in the wall will save you hours of tapping.

2. **Delegate to an equal.** Give the job to someone who is just as qualified as you. He or she can do it just as well as you can. It will take minimal time on your part to explain the job and give guidance.

3. **Delegate to a beginner.** Give the job to someone who doesn't know how to do it as well as you do. This requires the biggest investment of your time, as you will have to train and supervise, but there are great rewards. You become a mentor, and you earn yourself a grateful helper. For example, at work, you might delegate some of your creative work, such as writing descriptive copy or your monthly letter to clients, to your assistant. You will have to do some training, but once you've made that initial investment and your helper has completed the job, you can be glad that you have given someone else a chance to shine, enhanced that person's confidence in his or her abilities, and maybe even freed yourself up long-term.

Your goal is to assign each person to the job in which he or she can make the best possible contribution to the project. Consider your team members' talents, skills, vision, and availability. As you look over each task that needs to be done, ask yourself:

- Who is good at this?
- Who might enjoy this, or at least certain parts of this?
- Who might want to learn about this?
- Who is available?

Also consider how much time you will have to oversee the employee at work on the project; the less time you have to supervise, the more expert the team member will have to be.

At home, your team includes all your family members. However, if you have tasks that extend beyond the availability or talents of your family, you can also enlist others. Take advantage of delivery services. Hire a housekeeper or gardener, or a teenager to run errands. If you can't afford to hire help, you can barter with friends and neighbors. Some neighborhoods have created cooking co-ops that save all the members a lot of work while at the same time building community. The point is not to limit yourself to the obvious candidates.

The same holds true in the workplace. A common mistake managers make is that they often limit themselves to their staff, when in some cases, getting outside help would be more efficient and cost-effective. Hire outsiders when:

- **The project requires special expertise.** For example, if your office needs an overhaul of its computer system, don't add to the workload of your already overloaded employee who may not have much experience with computers. It could take significantly longer and yield poor results. Hire an expert from the outside.

- **The project requires little skill.** Don't pull your high-level administrative assistant off his or her important duties to spend four months sorting through old files or inputting data onto a computer when it's likely to take a huge amount of time. Hire a low-cost temp.

- **When the staff is already working to capacity**. After you have asked the questions, "Does this need to be done?"; "Does this need to be done now?" and "Can we reduce it or simplify it?" if you have work left over, hire appropriate outside help.

The Three Stages of Delegation

There are three stages of delegation. You need to budget time for all three stages.

- Stage 1: Present the job.
- Stage 2: Be available for guidance while the job is being done.
- Stage 3: Review and evaluate the end result.

STAGE 1: PRESENT THE JOB. People especially like to help when they feel they are making a valuable contribution to a goal. When you give assignments, let the people you're delegating to know that they are an important part of the team. Explain how the job contributes to the big picture, and how their part in it is necessary.

Talk to your helpers about what your objective is, but *don't* dictate in minutiae how they should perform their tasks. Make the goal measurable and specific, and give guidance and suggestions on methodology, but ultimately you should let the other people participate in deciding how they accomplish in the goal. It can be difficult to let go of your need to have it done your way, and you may have trouble understanding another person's approach, but the pride the person feels in making a contribution and the time you save yourself will be worth it.

Engage your team members' thoughts and creativity. When you

don't allow people enough room to make their own unique contributions to their work, everyone suffers. They feel sapped of energy and demoralized because they are being treated like automatons, and you lose out on the opportunity to tap into the fresh approach they may have had.

If you are delegating to someone who is not as seasoned as you are, his or her fresh approach may solve more problems than you think. Margarite hired a student intern to do data entry from her Website to her contact manager. A tedious chore, the student found a utility called Web Grabber, which sped up the process ten times over. If you delegate to equals or experts, their approach may teach you a thing or two as well. What's more, delegating the task while allowing one to come up with a personal approach brings dignity to the process and gives a chance for self-expression—a great motivator.

Also, be sure to give people an accurate time estimate. How much time are you asking of them? How do these tasks fit into their current schedules? Give them a deadline, and leave enough of a cushion so that if the work comes back to you in need of improvement, there is time to fix it before the real deadline.

STAGE 2: BE AVAILABLE WHILE THE JOB IS BEING DONE. Keep in mind that people who are doing projects for you will need guidance. You can either schedule regular times for your helpers to report to you, or you can respond to requests on an as-needed basis. This will vary, based on the person and the assignment, and should be determined at the outset of the job.

If the job is large and the stakes are high, it will make sense to schedule progress reports along the way so you can ensure that the job stays on course. For minor or low-stakes jobs, let your helper come to you if and when your input is needed. Plan to make time for progress reports so you don't feel frazzled by being continually interrupted by questions from your team member.

STAGE 3: REVIEW AND EVALUATE THE RESULT. After a delegated job has been completed, evaluate whether the result fulfills your goals. If it does, resist the urge to be a perfectionist and think about how if it had been you doing it, the margins would have been a half-inch wider, or the shirts would have been folded so that the creases fell in a less noticeable place. Celebrate the fact that you've just saved yourself a lot of time. Then reflect a little your team member's skills and talents so that next time you can give him or her more guidance if necessary, or choose to delegate the task to someone else if you're not happy with the outcome.

Dorie's seven-year-old son had just washed the lunch dishes. Dorie examined them and said, "They're wonderfully clean! Great job!" Since she was more concerned with teaching him a new skill than with having gleaming dishes, she saved her critical comments for the next time. The following week when she helped him get ready to wash the dishes again, she said, "You did such a nice job last week. This week you might get the dishes even cleaner if you used soap!"

If you've established that you're pleased with the results, talk to your team member about what he or she did well, what you liked, what you see as a special talent or unique solution, and how the person's work will help the project. If some changes are needed, try not to fix the problem yourself (which would require scheduling an extra large cushion of time before the deadline) or to rush to tell your helper how to fix it. Remind him or her what the goal was, and say, "This is close, but it doesn't seem to quite hit the mark. Do you have any suggestions about what we can do to get it there?" Let your helper be the problem solver. This respectful approach will help your team member to improve his or her skills and empower him.

Delegating at Home

The difference between delegating at work and at home is that at work, people have been hired for specific skills and so have certain areas of expertise that can guide you in selecting what to delegate to them. In a family, you don't get to interview your "employees" and hire them based on their qualifications—and you can't fire and replace them. This means you need to study the team you have, and try to discover and develop their individual strengths and weaknesses.

It's important that everyone in the family keep in mind the family's big-picture goals. Kids should remember that they aren't taking out the garbage or washing the car just to please Mom or Dad (or to keep you from scolding them), but because they are part of the family team. You all share the goal of an evenly distributed workload and achieving a home environment that is safe, clean, and inviting. In fact, some families even create a mission statement, to which every family member can commit, which spells out the family's goals.

At home, the fact that you don't get to select your team members means that you have more training to do. However, it is worth the investment. When the whole family contributes to the work of running the household, it brings you closer together. Your kids will learn skills that will benefit them in adulthood. It will also take some of the pressure off you. If you're trying to do it all, and that makes you feel constantly overloaded and overwhelmed, you are not going to have enough energy to make your most important contribution to your family—providing love, listening, and showing an interest in each family member.

Chores Kids Can Do

2- to 3-year-olds	4- to 5-year-olds	6- to 7-year-olds
• place napkins on table	• begin to dress self	• take out garbage
• clear own plate	• brush teeth and hair	• write shopping list
• put toys away into bins labelled with pictures	• clear or set table (except sharp knives)	• gather items at supermarket
• put clothing in hamper	• make own bed with comforter	• set out breakfast
	• tidy up room	• water plants
	• help weeding	• put bike away

8- to 10-year-olds	11- to 12-year-olds	13 and up
• walk the dog	• sweep, vaccuum, and mop floors	• do own laundry
• wash dishes	• mow the lawn	• clean a bathroom
• put laundry away	• make salads	• food-shop
• make sandwiches	• heat soups	• run errands
• rake leaves	• answer phones and take messages	• cook simple meals
• wash car		• organize photo albums

As your kids grow, and as you and your spouse's own lives and jobs go through changes, you can adjust both the distribution of the labor and your overall goals. Sometimes people develop new interests, and their chores can reflect that. When a family member is going through an exceptionally demanding time at work or school, other family members can pick up the slack temporarily. However, be careful to restore the equilibrium as soon possible, or a temporary change might become permanent. To keep your schedule balanced you'll need to step back and look at your big-picture goals regularly.

Once you have completed the purge stage, you have eliminated all extraneous tasks and extra steps, and are ready to get to work. Now the question is, when will you, or your helpers, do the job? In "Assign a Home," you'll learn how to schedule these tasks into your days.

9

ASSIGN A HOME

Now that you have decided *what* you are going to do, and how long it will take, the next question to ask yourself is, "*When* am I going to do the task? Will I do it this week or next? Am I going to do it in its activity zone, or will I need to divert from my Time Map and make some trade-offs?"

Just as you must decide on a "home" for all the individual objects in your physical space, you will need to determine a specific home in your schedule for all the tasks you have decided to do. For this part of the SPACE process, you must pull out your planner and work with it. Ideally, you will try to funnel your tasks into the proper time zone and 80 percent of the time you actually can.

I know what you're probably thinking: "Yes, this is all very sensible in theory, but I live in the real world. I can't do everything according to my Time Map. I get demands and requests from people who want things done on their timetable, and I have to deal with crises and interruptions."

However, the key to this process is to recognize that in many cases you *do* have the power to decide when you will do things. Too often you feel like a victim, reacting instantly to every demand or idea that comes your way. This knee-jerk reaction is the result of getting caught up in other people's priorities, and not having a master plan (i.e., a Time Map) of your own. Without a "place" to funnel tasks, you may feel that if you don't do something immediately, you will probably never get to it. So you do it right away.

If you're always in a reactive mode, you'll not only feel out of control, you'll suffer tremendous losses of time and productivity. Doing things on *your* time, when you are ready, almost always saves time, because you are prepared and can get right to what's important.

When you "assign a home," *you* are in command of when you will do things. You can postpone reacting to certain tasks until you are ready. You won't mind making people (including yourself) wait to get to a task, because you know exactly when that task can be done, and are confident that it won't slip through the cracks.

EVERY ITEM IN ITS PLACE, EVERY TASK IN ITS ZONE

If you were organizing a music activity zone in a living room, you would designate shelf for the jazz CDs, another for the classical CDs, another for the reggae. You don't just toss them in haphazardly. Similarly, you must designate specific locations on your Time Map for all your to-dos. "Assigning a home" means that for any given task, you create a time slot within the proper activity zone—in other words, on which day and at what hour you will do it. Remember the kindergarten model: each activity zone of time contains specific tasks that relate to that activity.

For example, Zoë, a freelance writer, has established writing time every day from seven A.M. to eleven A.M. During the sort and purge stages, she decided which stories and articles she would write. During "Assign a Home," she determines which day she will work on each particular story. On Monday through Thursday, from seven A.M. to nine A.M., she will work on the Broadway review. From nine A.M. to eleven A.M., she'll work on the Charlie Parker article. On Friday from seven to eleven, she'll get started on the chamber music story.

Zoë not only assigns a home for these specific writing projects, she records them in her planner so that when she sits down to work she knows exactly what she is working on. If she gets an idea for a new article, she can tell at a glance that there's no room in her schedule this week. To find a "home" for that new writing task, she will have to switch off with another article or postpone the task for the next week. This way, she doesn't get distracted by all the possibilities of what to write. It's clear what she will write and when.

For every task you have chosen to do, you should block off the time in your planner for it. If the task is a quick phone call, it is enough simply to list it on the day you want to make it. However, if the task will take fifteen minutes or more, choose a specific *time* in which do it. In other words, I want you to schedule your to-dos as appointments with yourself.

Tuesday • September 5

SEPTEMBER 2000

S	M	T	W	T	F	S
					1	2
3	4	5	6	7	8	9
10	11	12	13	14	15	16
17	18	19	20	21	22	23
24	25	26	27	28	29	30

TO DO

TO DO

Absolutely DON'T forget

early am

8 *SELF—Wake up, make coffee, check e-mail.*

9 *FAMILY—Breakfast and shower routine with husband and baby.*

10 *FAMILY/WORK—Phone call to co-write/cleaning kitchen. Husband takes baby for day.*

11 *HOME—Neighborhood errands—grocery store, dry cleaners, drugstore. Put away groceries, laundry and pur-*

12 *chases, file receipts, check in with husband.*

1 *SELF—Lunch. Bike ride.*

2 *FAMILY/FRIEND—Take care of baby for a few hours while straightening up and/or making personal*

3 *calls.*

4

5 *FAMILY—Dinner prep, eating, and cleanup.*

6 *FAMILY—Pick up clutter and start hand washing.*

7 *FAMILY—Watch movie with husband, hand-washing, playing with baby.*

8

9 *FAMILY—Put baby to bed. Relationship Time.*

10 *Time with husband. SELF—Journal writing. Bed.*

late pm

A home weekend to-do list. I've noted here the categories for all these tasks, but you don't need to do this when making out your own list.

February 2000
24 HOUR SCHEDULE

FEBRUARY 2000

S	M	T	W	T	F	S
		1	2	3	4	5
6	7	8	9	10	11	12
13	14	15	16	17	18	19
20	21	22	23	24	25	26
27	28	29				

7 AM

CLIENT MATTERS —
Smith case

8

9 COMMUTE — proof
reading

10
OPEN — calls*

11 CLIENT MATTERS —
Jones Case

12 NOON
LUNCH — Working
at desk

1 MEETING W/CLIENTS
· Ward

2 · Shapiro

3 CLIENT MATTERS —
Wells case

4 OPEN — calls

5

6 COMMUTE — reading
professional journals

7 PM

8

9 *Calls to make —
Blahno

10 Marvin
Kathy R.
Tax commissioner

11

12 MIDNIGHT
*e-mail —
Respond to Bill Z.
Soap Company
Stats to Laura R.
Sanders' Comptroller

1

2

3

4

5

A lawyer's work to-do list. Note that the list of calls and e-mails for the day are in the right column; these will be made during one of the three time slots for calls and e-mails.

Time Boundaries

Some people feel confined when they schedule everything down to the smallest increment of time, while others feel more confident that they will stay on track if they know what they are doing in any given half-hour time block. Your activity zones can be as personalized as a dresser drawer—some people are most comfortable with their socks carefully separated from each other by plastic dividers, while others are fine just knowing that all their socks are in one place. Remember, your Time Map is customizable to your personal style.

If your "Natural Rhythms and Habits Self-Test" in chapter 3 revealed that you thrive on a lot of structure, you may always want to assign a specific time to each phone call, letter, and project. If, on the other hand, the self-test showed that you thrive on flexibility, you might simply want to say, "I'll make phone calls from nine to eleven A.M. Here are the eight calls I want to make, and I'll make them in any order that feels right to me at the time."

I strongly recommend assigning a specific time limit for each task when you are just getting started with this method. It will help you become a better calculator. It also forces you to place a relative value on each task—how much time do you really want to spend on it? Then, as you master the technique, adjust it to work with your personal style. You want the system to be firm enough to provide a structure that enables you to achieve your goals, but you don't want it to be so rigid that it becomes cumbersome or unrealistic.

Arranging Tasks in Your Time Map Activity Zones

When you place your tasks within an activity zone, lay them out in a way that feels natural to you. If you're having trouble, you might consider grouping them:

BY URGENCY. Even if you have plenty of time to accomplish all your tasks in that activity zone, if you get the most important task or two done first, you'll feel a sense of accomplishment and be energized to keep going.

BY DURATION OF THE TASK. If you have fifteen phone calls to make in an hour, and you know that some of the people you're calling tend to be long-winded, you might want to leave those calls for last so that you have less time available for indulging them.

BY ENERGY OR INTEREST LEVEL. If some tasks are more difficult than others, you may want to get them out of the way first so that you have plenty of energy to get to the easier tasks. Tackling the unpleasant tasks first will leave you energized and ready for the fun tasks.

BY GEOGRAPHY. If you are running errands, you could run the mall errands and then all the errands that require travel to the other side of town.

Experiment with different ways of grouping your tasks. You may hit upon an order that inspires you to be your most productive.

The important thing is that you get to your tasks when you planned to get to them.

TRADE-OFFS

Of course, there will be times when you just can't funnel a task into the correct activity zone on your Time Map and you have to attend to it sooner rather than later. For example, let's revisit the situation from chapter 7, "Sort," in which your son Jason wants you to take him to the mall to buy the soccer cleats you promised him. You use Saturday afternoons for family errands, and Saturday afternoon is coming up in three days, but unfortunately, Jason's game is tomorrow so he needs the shoes today.

Of course, you can tell Jason you are unavailable and have someone else take him, or streamline the task by ordering some shoes on-line. But if none of these solutions works for you, you'll have to consult your Time Map and see if you can make a trade-off.

Time	Monday	Tuesday	Wednesday	Thursday	Friday	Saturday
12 noon to 3 P.M.						family time
6 P.M. to 8 P.M.			study time			
8 P.M. to 10 P.M.				self time		

STUDY/SELF/FAMILY MAP 1

If you take Jason to the mall tonight at six you won't have time to study for the continuing education course you're taking; if you take him tomorrow night after eight you'll cut into your self time.

Maybe you can trade your study time or self time to Saturday afternoon. If so, you can take Jason shopping when he needs to go, without sacrificing something important to you.

Time	Monday	Tuesday	Wednesday	Thursday	Friday	Saturday
12 noon to 3 P.M.						study time
6 P.M. to 8 P.M.			family time			
8 P.M. to 10 P.M.				self time		

STUDY/SELF/FAMILY MAP 2

If an exact swap isn't possible, try to juggle your schedule a little. Let's say you can't make up the time on Saturday because you have already purchased tickets to spend family time seeing a matinee. Maybe you can move studying to your self time this week and make up for it next week by scheduling a little extra self time.

Time	Monday	Tuesday	Wednesday	Thursday	Friday	Saturday
12 noon to 3 P.M.						family time
6 P.M. to 8 P.M.			family time			
8 P.M. to 10 P.M.				study time		

STUDY/SELF/FAMILY MAP 3

You have a lot of flexibility when you work with your Time Map. The most important thing is to be aware of the trade-offs you are making, and always strive to regain the balance you have set for yourself.

RESPECTING YOUR TIME MAP

While your Time Map can be flexible, I strongly encourage you to *think of the time you've blocked out for your to-dos as if they were appointments with important business clients.* That means not rushing to cancel them when something else comes up. Tell people, "I'm sorry, I have an appointment"—they don't have to know it's an appointment with yourself to indulge in your hobby for two hours. Similarly, at work, you need to communicate clearly when you are unavailable due to work scheduled. If you like, you can tell people that two to three is your time to catch up on paperwork, but sometimes the less said the better—you shouldn't have to defend the way you have structured your time.

At this point, you've put a lot of thought into what you want to do and when. It's important to stick to your plan. That means starting and stopping tasks when you planned to. How do you do this? By learning to "containerize" tasks—that is, prevent one task from spilling over into the next. In the next chapter, you'll learn more about staying on track by overcoming procrastination, conquering chronic lateness, and managing interruptions, all of which are the big enemies to sticking to your schedule.

10

CONTAINERIZE

Plan your work, and then work your plan.

Now that you've assigned a home to your tasks, it's time to master the art of "containerizing," that is, keeping tasks within the time you've allotted for them. No procrastination, no letting tasks drag on endlessly. Once you've learned how to containerize, you will find yourself moving buoyantly through your to-do list and feeling a wonderful sense of satisfaction every day.

Containerizing is a critical skill that all the best time managers have mastered. They make swift decisions. They don't procrastinate. They are rarely late. They do exactly what they plan to do, when they plan to do it, with little hesitation. Because they get their to-dos done in the time they have allotted for them, they move through their days feeling energized, optimistic, and satisfied.

So how do you containerize time? In three ways:

1. Minimizing interruptions and their impact
2. Conquering procrastination and chronic lateness
3. Overcoming perfectionism

MINIMIZING INTERRUPTIONS AND THEIR IMPACT

Interruptions and crises will always happen, and most of them will feel *urgent,* but of course, not every interruption is indeed a crisis. It's tempting to react to interruptions instantly, especially since the people who interrupt you can be very demanding. But if you stop to handle every interruption the minute it comes up, you will be pulled in many different directions, become confused and overwhelmed, and end up neglecting your own plans. You can learn to minimize interruptions, whether they are external (caused by other people) or internal (your own need to switch gears).

Defer Your Response

It's important to realize that most crises really aren't crises. When people come to you with so-called urgent demands, the very first thing to do is consider what is at stake if you don't respond immediately. In most cases, you can postpone your response for at least a few minutes and often longer without causing any disasters, so go ahead and take some time. This breathing space will enable you to attack the problem in action-mode, rather than reaction mode. You'll be able to put the task through the sort, purge, and assign processes, which will save you much-needed time and energy.

No matter how precisely you plan your agenda, however, try not to schedule it so tightly that you have no room to handle any interruptions or crises that undoubtedly will arise. The amount of time you should leave open will vary depending on what you do. Look honestly at the demands of your job and your life, and begin to set up systems to allow for the amount of interruptions you must face.

If your job requires you to handle a huge volume of phone calls, for example, you may need to allow six hours of unplanned time each day to take your calls, and be able to plan only two hours of concentrated work. It may be only two hours, but two uninterrupted hours are probably far more productive than the same amount of time spread out over the day, broken up by phone calls.

Reduce Interruptions

Here are some ways to minimize the most common external interruptions encountered at work and at home.

• **If you're in an open cubicle at work, turn your desk or your chair away from the open area to avoid easy eye contact.** If that's not possible, place some plants on the periphery of your desk as a boundary between you and your environment. People are less likely to interrupt when they can't make eye contact first.

• **Establish visiting hours.** Put up a sign on your office door saying "Please do not disturb until 3:00," or tell your people that you can't talk to anyone between two and three o'clock. Some companies are establishing a quiet hour once a day, in which all the phones are put on voice mail and people can have an uninterrupted hour for concentrated working.

• **Wear earplugs.**

- **Establish a set time each day when you will get back to callers.** Let someone else take your calls, or have your voice mail take a message. For this to work, you have to call people back when you promise you will. Also, you tend to be more efficient when *you* make the call—the average incoming phone call takes eleven minutes, the average outgoing call takes only seven. That's because you've had the time to gather your thoughts.

- **Set aside regular, specific times of day to handle your mail, voice mail, and e-mail.** You may have to speak to your boss or co-workers about the need to limit the number of times you check your e-mail.

- **Recycle or toss junk mail without opening it and take yourself off junk mail lists.** Write to Mail Preference Services, P.O. Box 9008, Farmingdale, NY 11735 to get your name off of junk mail lists. Write to Telephone Preference Services, P.O. Box 9014, Farmingdale, NY 11735.

- **Set up your e-mail program to delete messages that come in from known spammers (people who send junk e-mail).** You can also set up your e-mail program so that it directs messages with certain words or phrases such as "Money Making Opportunity" or "XXX" directly into the trash.

- **Whenever possible, respond to e-mails with a quick "Yes," "Will do," or "Thanks!"** If responding to an e-mail requires a lot of thought, work, or research, send a quick response letting the sender know you received the e-mail and are working on it.

- **To avoid obtrusive instant messages when researching online, log on with a different e-mail name.** Use an alternate e-mail name that only you know or set your computer to block the retrieval of all IMs or just some. And be respectful of others' time, too; don't assume that if someone's on-line they have time for a conversation with you.

• **To limit junk e-mail, post on message boards using a secondary e-mail name.** "Spammers" get e-mail addresses from postings. If you must post, create an e-mail name especially for this function; all the e-mail you receive under that name will be junk e-mail or responses to your posts, and you won't have to sort through it on your main e-mail account.

• **Schedule regular meeting times for communication.** If you work closely with someone, or need to check in with your spouse and kids, a planned, short meeting once or twice a day can be one of the best time savers in the world—no more having to interrupt each other every ten minutes to exchange information.

• **Use project reports.** If you work on projects with other people, create a daily or weekly "ongoing projects report" so that everyone can easily check the status of the project without interrupting each other. At home or at the office, you might also plan regular "update" meetings, in person or on the phone.

SAMPLE ONGOING PROJECTS REPORT

Project	Contact	Deadline	Documents	Next Step
Northern Park Mall	Dana	December 3	See "Northern Park Mall" folder	Dana will contact the developers on November 25

INTERNAL INTERRUPTIONS

Of course, it isn't always *someone else* who interrupts you. Sometimes we interrupt ourselves, and this can be just as counterproductive. Here are some suggestions for minimizing these internal interruptions.

• **Prepare snacks ahead of time and eat before you start.** Rather than going without food for long stretches, or running to the vending machine for a candy bar to tide you over, invest a few minutes in preparing some snacks before you start a long project. Bring a bottle of water to your desk, or keep a Thermos bottle of coffee in your office.

• **Keep your planner accessible at all times for jotting down thoughts that come to mind.** When you don't have a single, consistent place to record the new to-dos that you think of, or ideas you want to follow up on, it's really tempting to jump up and do them right away. Yet if you create a safe, reliable place to record this information, you can fight this temptation. Keep your planner nearby and record ideas as they occur to you. At work, everyone should bring their planners to meetings so that they can record new notes to themselves. One company created a notebook called "The Parking Lot," in which they record nonagenda items that come up during meetings, which they can address at another time.

• **Keep a notebook or tape recorder on hand to record more complex ideas.** Creative people often need more space for recording their sudden inspirations than a planner can provide, or they need a different medium. Consistently carry a tape recorder to record musical ideas, or a notebook in which you can actually draw and sketch, if you find these helpful.

• **Plan for a seventh-inning stretch.** You will need to get up every so often and stretch—unless you want to grow into the shape of your chair. Just be sure to plan for taking ten minutes out of every hour to stretch, or whatever feels right for you, and then get back to work.

CONQUERING PROCRASTINATION AND CHRONIC LATENESS

Procrastination and chronic lateness often go hand in hand and are often caused by the same issues. Therefore, the solutions to each are very similar.

Procrastination

In my experience, once people have gotten to the "containerize" stage of this program, procrastination becomes less of an issue. Since you have gone through the process of defining your goals and creating a Time Map, you have a higher appreciation of the value of your time. You feel inspired and motivated to finish each task on your to-do list because you know it is connected to one of your big-picture goals, and you are excited about moving on to the next task on your list. However, there will still be times when you find yourself having a hard time moving through your day.

Procrastination is the biggest enemy of a successfully planned day. When you get a late start, it can make one activity spill over into the time allotted for the next activity, causing a domino effect that leaves many items on your to-do list undone. To compound the problem, when you procrastinate, you often end up distracting yourself by doing insignificant tasks that are not connected to your goals, so the time spent procrastinating is truly a waste.

One of the worst effects of procrastination is the energy drain that results. You spend a lot of time feeling like a failure for not accomplishing what you need to accomplish, and this steals even more time and energy from your ability to move on to the next thing on your to-do list.

If you are procrastinating, it's *not* because you are lazy or irresponsible. There are many causes for procrastination, and many of them are simple to fix.

First, ask yourself whether you procrastinate on only *some* tasks, or on practically *everything*. If you procrastinate on only some tasks, you're probably making a technical error, that is, there's something about these specific tasks or the way that you are approaching them that is causing the delay. If you procrastinate about everything, it's likely that your motives are psychologically based—take a look back at the psychological obstacles section in chapter 2, "What's Holding You Back?" Pay particular attention to psychological obstacles: #2, Conquistador of Chaos; #5, Fear of Failure; #6, Fear of Success; and #8, Fear of Completion. Meanwhile, here is some guidance on overcoming the most common technical causes of procrastination.

FEELING INDECISIVE. One way of procrastinating is to put off making a decision. Good time managers know that making swift decisions is a big part of completing projects and staying on schedule.

So how do you make good decisions quickly? By trusting your instincts and keeping your eye on the big picture. When you have your goals in mind, you recognize that each task is only one aspect of a larger plan, and that no one decision is going to make or break your success. It's a very liberating realization, and it makes it easier to move quickly through the decisions you have to make. If you're procrastinating about a decision, ask yourself what your big-picture goal is. Most of the time, this will put things quickly in perspective and help you to make the right decision.

NOT BEING READY. Sometimes, you procrastinate because you really aren't ready to do a particular task. You may not have all the information you need to make a decision yet, or you may not be prepared for the outcome the project will produce.

For example, you may be procrastinating about hiring a new employee because you aren't really ready to commit to another salary right now. You may be procrastinating on submitting a proposal because you feel you are lacking certain skills to deliver the job well. Honestly examine whether you are ready to deal with the results of completing a task—and if you aren't, give yourself permission to back off for now.

If you aren't ready to tackle a particular task, what you can do is focus your efforts on steps that will get you ready. If you are putting off hiring an assistant because you aren't ready for the additional expense, your next step could be to reanalyze your profit margin or add another revenue stream. If you are postponing that proposal because of a skill you lack, try taking a course or reading up on that skill as your next step.

FEELING OVERWHELMED. Some tasks and projects are so complex that you don't know how to get started. Or maybe you do know how to get started, but the project is very big and the results seem very far away. Maybe you have ten years' worth of old papers to sort or a novel to write.

Break down overwhelming tasks into manageable parts. Instead of facing one huge, amorphous task looming ominously over your head, divide of it into three (or six, or ten) achievable steps. Each step could be one hour, or one day in duration. Then concentrate only the first step.

Sometimes the size or difficulty of a project feels paralyzing. In that case adopting a phrase or ditty to motivate yourself to just get started may be all you need. A lot of people think "Just do it", "Do it now!", or "If not now, when?" I think of a Mr. Rogers song "You've got to do it, just do it." I heard it one day watching the show with my daughter when she was little. It's very simple and is just what I need to get me past any moments of hesitation.

Once you are in motion, everything changes. You are engaged and connected. You feel the wind in your face and you feel better about yourself. You'll be surprised how your energy and momentum build, and before you know it, you will be enjoying the journey.

HATING THE TASK. Often, we procrastinate because, frankly, we just loathe the task. Don't beat yourself up for being undisciplined.

Delegate it! Maybe you can hire someone. You'd be surprised at some of the services available—you can hire people to organize your photo albums, walk your dog, pack a picnic or cook Thanksgiving dinner, childproof your home, or file your health insurance claims. You can even hire people to do a part of a task: there are interior decorators who will simply come in and give you an opinion, and catering services that will bring you just the Thanksgiving turkey and leave the cranberry sauce to you. You can also barter with your spouse or a neighbor—trade a task you hate for a task he or she hates.

What if it's a task you can't delegate, such as exercising or going to the dentist? In this case, find a way to make the task more enjoyable, and it will give you the edge you need to win the procrastination tug-of-war with yourself. Combine it with something you absolutely love to do. If you hate to exercise, ride your exercise bike while watching your favorite television show, read while walking on a treadmill, go to the gym with a friend whose company you love, or go inline skating with your kids.

You might be motivated to carry out a dreaded task if you bribe yourself. Schedule a manicure immediately following every dentist's appointment. Read a junk magazine (the kind you are embarrassed to enjoy) whenever you go to the dentist—and only when you go to the dentist.

It also helps to focus on your goals. When you keep your eye on the benefits of the task, rather than on the dreaded task itself, it can make any process more tolerable.

Finally, you can always give your task a very short time limit. Split the job if you can: if it takes thirty minutes to pay your bills each month and you find it torturous, spread it out over two fifteen-minute sessions instead of one long, grueling one. Knowing the torture won't go on forever will help you to stop procrastinating. You may even be encouraged to get the job done before your time is up.

BAD TIMING. In chapter 3 you read about honoring your own unique personal rhythms and energy. When you recognize and respect your own peak times for various activities, you can overcome the procrastination that is caused by doing a task at the wrong time. If you can't get motivated to clean your house after working all day, clean it on the weekends, or in the morning, when you're feeling energetic.

NEED FOR PRESSURE. Many people really do work better under pressure. When they're working with a deadline hanging over them, they are freed from a certain level of perfectionism. Which permits them to lighten up, stop worrying, and just do it.

If leaving everything to the last minute truly helps you perform better, the first step is to accept this about yourself. Then establish self-imposed deadlines in advance of the actual deadline. If you have a proposal due on Friday, make your deadline three days earlier. Then book other urgent matters in the days following the proposal. This keeps you under pressure, but builds in a three-day cushion in case anything really goes wrong. You'll be safe.

In my experience, most people who adopt this "false deadline" technique eventually outgrow the need to do things at the last minute. After a while, they discover how liberating it is to have things done a few days in advance and then they begin to enjoy getting things done ahead of time.

Overcoming Chronic Lateness

What if you're always late? When you are perpetually behind schedule, you end up ruining your plans. You arrive twenty minutes late to a meeting and feel terribly embarrassed. You spend ten minutes apologizing, and the next fifteen distracted by thoughts of guilt and self-criticism, inwardly chanting a mantra about how you'll never be late again.

Chronic lateness throws you off schedule just as procrastination does. Moreover, it's demoralizing to have to constantly apologize, and scold yourself. Many of the techniques for dealing with procrastination will help you overcome lateness as well, but there are some elements unique to lateness that should be addressed separately.

Even though chronically late people are frequently accused of being rude, I don't believe they ever intend to be rude to others. They're just so lost in their own chaos that it doesn't occur to them that other people might be adversely affected by their lateness. It's only after the habitually tardy recover from their chronic lateness that they realize how inconsiderate their behavior must have seemed to the people left waiting.

If you are struggling with chronic lateness, you are trying your best to be on time, but something is standing in your way. In order to pinpoint the reason for your lateness, ask yourself, "Am I always late by *different* amounts of time or am I always late by the *same* amount of time?" If you are always late by *different* amounts of time, chances are you are making purely technical errors—that is, it's hard for you to calculate accurately how long things take. See chapter 7, "Sort," for help with being a better calculator. On the other hand, if you are always late by the *same* amount of time (e.g., you're always fifteen minutes late), you're most likely up against a psychological obstacle (see chapter 2, "What's Holding You Back?"). Pay particular attention Psychological Obstacle #2: Conquistador of Chaos and #3: Fear of Downtime.

If the problem is that you're not good at calculating how long things take to do, the solution is to learn to be a better time estimator, using the techniques I suggested in chapter 7. Until you get better at estimating how long tasks take, build in a cushion of time for yourself before appointments. Plan to get there fifteen minutes early and catch up on a little reading while you wait. Set your clocks ahead ten minutes and act as if they showed the real time.

If what delays you from leaving on time is that you keep getting distracted on your way out the door turn back to the section on handling interruptions, located earlier in this chapter. Remember, handling interruptions is a critical skill for containerizing time, and keeping to your plans.

OVERCOMING PERFECTIONISM

If you really want to containerize tasks, you have to conquer the need for perfection. It can be hard to let go of a task, especially if it's an important one or you've gotten into the "groove" of it. As you're cleaning the bathroom, you realize it would look even better if you went a little further and scrubbed the grout. As you're writing the letter, you think of a better way to word it, and a better way, and a better way. Soon, you find yourself running overtime.

Mastering the art of containerizing means learning when to let go of your need for perfectionism so that tasks don't drag on and on. To put a task in perspective, step back for a moment and ask yourself how much difference a little more polishing is going to make. Will expanding this task force you to take time away from another important activity?

To prevent tasks from expanding unnecessarily, give yourself a clear deadline and schedule another task right after it. If you say, "I have to write a letter, and I'm just going to write it until it's done," it will generally take you a lot longer to do it than if you say, "I'm going to write this letter in half an hour and then I'm going to call Joe and discuss that new client." You will keep yourself *really* on track by writing in your planner, "2:30–3:00 P.M.: Write letter. 3:00–3:15 P.M.: Talk to Joe."

Deadlines may create pressure, but they can also be a blessing. Lee, a radio anchor for an all-news station, says that without strict deadlines, no news would ever make it onto the air. The writers would keep writing and rewriting, perfecting and polishing stories forever.

Deadlines force you to make decisions and to limit your need for perfectionism. When you have something waiting for you on the other side of the deadline, you're much more inspired to get the first thing done and move on to the next.

As you get more used to working with your Time Map, you will find it easier to remember that expanding a task in order to fiddle with it more will force you to make trade-offs you might not want to make.

At this point, you have sorted, purged, assigned a home, and containerized. Your days are filled with meaningful tasks that are helping you achieve your big-picture goals. Life feels good. You are in control. What's left? Equalize. In chapter 11, you will learn how to keep the balance in your life over time and accommodate the daily, periodic, and long-term crises that can throw you off schedule.

11

EQUALIZE

Time management is not a stagnant process. It is a constant inter-action between you, your goals, and the constantly changing rhythms and tempos of life. Life is full of surprises, and the ride can be fun, if you have a plan and a way to react and adapt.

That's what equalizing is: monitoring your situation and then making adjustments that keep you on track. When it comes to time management, you need to equalize daily, bimonthly, and whenever your schedule gets thrown off track. Keeping your balance even when your life takes unexpected turns is an art.

Daily Monitoring

In order to stay on track (or at least know how far off track you are), you need to review your planner at least twice each day, once in the morning and again at the end of the day. In addition, you will need to keep your eye on it throughout the day if your schedule is especially busy or contains a wide variety of activities.

At the end of each day, equalize your schedule by doing an evening cleanup of your Time Map. Review your to-do list, and check off everything you got done. Examine the tasks you didn't get to, and think about whether you can delete any of them. A task that was critical in the morning may be irrelevant by the evening. For example, you might have intended to write an important proposal to win over a potential client, but in the meantime your prospect called and placed an order, so now you can cross that task off your list.

Tasks you still want to do should be moved forward in your planner. Look over the next few days in your schedule and decide when you will get to them, then record them on the designated day.

I often like to put an open circle "O" to the left of any items I didn't get to, just to give myself a visual picture of the ratio of items "done" versus those "not done" on a given day. This keeps me honest about my time management and helps me to improve; I am constantly refining my own skills of estimating how long things take, delegating, and planning realistically.

Bimonthly Tune-Ups and Other Adjustments

Because life moves so rapidly and changes so quickly, to manage your time, you should plan a tune-up on a bimonthly basis. Your Time Map ought to reflect your current goals, priorities, and interests. Every two months, review your Time Map to make sure it supports your current goals. You may need to expand the time allotted for one activity, and shrink the time allotted for another.

Though your big-picture goals will rarely change, the activities you choose to support these goals will change over time. Every two months, review your activities and see whether they still warrant a place in your schedule. You may have achieved some of your specific objectives, or your priorities may have shifted.

Also, keep in mind that whenever you go through a major life change, you'll have to revamp your Time Map. When you have a baby, you will have to accommodate your little one into your schedule, while still leaving time for yourself and for your relationship with your spouse. A new job will require an adjustment; perhaps you will have more interruptions from clients, or more meetings to attend than before. If you marry, go back to school, or even just discover a new interest that you really want to pursue, you will need to fit new activities into your Time Map, adjust the time allotted for other activities, and maybe move a few things around.

How to Equalize During Times of Crisis

There are times in everyone's life when several crises hit you at once and multiple priorities converge. No matter how organized and balanced you have become under normal circumstances, occasionally you will find yourself in a situation where everything is urgent, time sensitive, and deadline driven. In these situations, you need to readjust your attack. Faced with such an onslaught, your impulse may be to jump into reaction mode, answering whatever screams loudest at any given moment. However, this is not the best approach.

The first thing you need to do is to step back from the chaos. You need to gather your thoughts and analyze the situation, and this is best done with a little distance. If it's at all possible, get some physical distance between yourself and the situation. Take a walk, a drive, a shower, or go to the gym. A regrouping moment will enable you to get out of the details, rise above the panic, and start to make good decisions. Your goal is to come up with a plan of action that spells out exactly what to do and when to do it, so that you get to everything important.

Apply the SPACE formula. Sort all the tasks that are confronting you. *Purge whatever you can.* Ask yourself which tasks you can delete or shortcuts you can create. Also, consider whether you can delegate any of these tasks or any portions of the tasks. When life is this hectic, you need to keep your sanity and energy for the things that matter most. Assign a home on your Time Map only to those most critical activities.

You will have to forgo certain routine activities for a while. You may not be able to cook healthy dinners or get the car washed during this time. Accept that, and don't feel guilty about it.

Even if you are the type of person who thrives on flexibility, when everything is urgent, you will have to structure your time tightly. Schedule appointments with yourself for every task on your to-do list. This will keep you focused and productive, and will prevent any one task from monopolizing your time—something you cannot afford when there is so much pressure on you.

Your plan will also allow you to concentrate on just the moment you are in. When you map out where and how you will spend your time, giving each activity a place in your schedule, you no longer have to worry about how you will fit everything in. You've already decided that, and you are free to focus on whatever you are doing at the moment.

No matter how intense things get, make sure that you always preserve some time for self-renewal. Decide which activity most effectively recharges you (going to the gym, getting a massage, making love), and make time for it. It will give you the strength you need to get through the crisis. Take care of yourself: eat well, get enough rest and enough exercise. Select one regular activity from each of the other critical departments of your life (reading to your kids, taking a walk with your mate, speaking with your friends), and fit that in. Then let everything else go and focus on the crisis.

Get back to your ideal balance as soon as you can. When the crisis is over, you may need to spend a few weeks compensating for the things you were unable to get to during that time.

However, be aware that sometimes crises like these require a permanent adjustment of your Time Map because your circumstances have changed permanently. After each crisis, evaluate your Time Map to see if it needs to be adjusted.

Forgive Yourself for Your Failures

If you don't get to everything you wanted to get to in any given day or during a crisis, don't beat yourself up. Very few people ever finish every last thing on their to-do lists. As long as you are regularly getting to all the important things in your life, you don't have to worry that you haven't gotten to every single item.

Because life changes so frequently, your priorities may change with it. Your moods are not static, and your energy levels will fluctuate. A project you may have thought would be almost effortless turns out to be very difficult and draining, which will in turn influence how you function for the rest of the week. There are circumstances that may distract you—relationship problems, illnesses. There are also circumstances that energize you—you might fall in love and suddenly have enough energy and confidence to tackle two days' worth of tasks in one morning. Give yourself room to ride those waves, and always keep your eye on your planner so that you can make adjustments.

The worst thing to do is berate yourself for not getting everything done, for periodically procrastinating, and for slowing down from time to time. The time and energy you spend feeling guilty create a downward spiral of nonproductivity. Even the most productive people occasionally have off days. The thing that makes them good time managers is that they realize these things are a part of life, forgive themselves, make the necessary adjustments to their schedules, and move on.

If you have an off day, take a few moments to analyze what went wrong. Were you overbooked, underbooked, too tired, or especially stressed? Was there an event that caused you to disregard your plans? Can you avoid this problem in the future?

The most liberating aspect of time management from the inside out is that it is a way of creating a life that nurtures you and makes you feel *good*. You are the master of your own life, and while you can't control all the events around you, you can control your reactions to those events. Instead of dwelling on what you haven't achieved, give yourself credit for what you have been able to do.

Celebrate Your Successes

Specific moments of achievement give us an opportunity to celebrate. So often we tend to gloss over those moments in our rush to move on to the next thing on the to-do list. When we do that, we cheat ourselves of one of the great pleasures in life.

Take time to celebrate your victories. Finally land a big contract you've worked your butt off to get? You have a clear-cut moment of triumph—whoop it up! Call a friend, break out the bubbly, buy yourself some theater tickets—do something fun and exhilarating. When you have goals and you're achieving them, you get a fabulous sense of accomplishment! Relish this feeling, and invite the people in your life to relish it with you. This will bolster your self-esteem, and it will invigorate you to go on achieving and enjoying.

When you implement the techniques in this book, at first it will feel like work. At some point, though, you will notice your time is under control and you are working toward goals that are meaningful to you—and achieving them. You will pick up momentum, and begin to feel full of confidence and in love with your life. This is the true meaning of success, and you should celebrate it!

Congratulations! You have learned a whole new approach to time management. The skills you have learned about in these pages will serve you for life, no matter what changes you go through as a person, or what surprises are in store for you.

In dancing, when the music changes, it often takes a little time to catch up with the rhythm of the new song. But if you hang in there, and stay focused on your partner and the music, before you know it you're back on the beat. The same is true of life. When life throws you curveballs, you will have brief periods of adjustment. But as long as you pay close attention to what you need and what your partner (time) is doing, you'll be back on an even footing in no time.

Time Management from the Inside Out is an extraordinary way of making the most of the life you have been given, and enjoying every step along the way. So don't hold back on the sidelines any longer. Get out there on the dance floor and dance! Give yourself permission to be who you are and go after your dreams. A wonderful, gratifying life awaits you.

Appendix

Sources for Time Management Products/Sources for Organizing Products

RESOURCES

Time Management Tools

At-A-Glance: ataglance.com (800) 302-4155

Day Runner: dayrunner.com (800) 232-9786

Day-Timer: daytimer.com (800) 225-5005

Franklin Covey: franklincovey.com (800) 842-2439

Filofax: filofax.com (203) 563-2200

Harold Taylor: taylorontime.com (800) 361-8463

PDAs/Palmtops/HPCs

Casio: www.casio.com (800) 962-2746

Hewlett-Packard: www.hp.com (800) 724-6631

Palm: www.palm.com (800) 881-7256

Psion: www.psion.com (978) 371-0310

Sharp: www.sharp-usa.om (800) BE-SHARP

Online Calendars, Schedulers, PIMs

These sites keep your personal or group calendar, scheduling, and contact information online.

AnyDay: anyday.com

Yahoo! Calendar: calendar.yahoo.com

Visto: visto.com

Online Software Resources

Read reviews or see screenshots, and download trial versions of PIMs and other helpful time-saving software.

SoftSeek: softseek.com

ZD Net: zdnet.com/downloads

CATALOGS AND STORES

Home

Bed, Bath and Beyond: bedbathandbeyond.com (800) GO-BEYOND

Container Store: containerstore.com (800) 733-3532

Exposures: exposuresonline.com (800) 572-5750

Frontgate: frontgate.com (800) 626-6488

Get Organized: getorginc.com (800) 803-9400

Hold Everything: holdeverything.com (800) 421-2264

Ikea: ikea.com (800) 434-4532

Lechters Housewares: lechtersonline.com (800) 60-KITCH

Levenger: levenger.com (800) 544-0880

Lillian Vernon: lillianvernon.com (800) 285-5555

Pottery Barn: potterybarn.com (800) 922-5507

Office/Home Office

Bindertek: bindertek.com (800) 456-3453

Ikea: ikea.com (888) 225-IKEA

Levenger: levenger.com (800) 544-0880

Mobile Office Outfitter: mobilegear.com (800) 426-3453

Office Depot: officedepot.com (800) 685-8800

Office Max: officemax.com (800) 788-8080

Quill: quillcorp.com (800) 789-1331

Reliable: reliable.com (800) 735-4000

Staples: staples.com (800) 333-3330

Local Office & Art Supplier: call for local number

ADDITIONAL RESOURCES

Public Storage Self-Storage (pickup and delivery): publicstorage .com (800) 44-STORE

The National Association of Professional Organizers—Information and Referral Hotline (for names of organizers in your area): napo.net (512) 206-0151

Julie Morgenstern Online: juliemorgenstern.com (212) 544-8722

Suggested Further Reading

TIME

Breathing Space, Jeff Davidson, MasterMedia, Ltd., 1991.

First Things First, Stephen R. Covey, A. Roger Merrill, and Rebecca R. Merrill, Simon & Schuster, 1994.

A Geography of Time, Robert Levine, Basic Books, 1997.

How to Take Control of Your Time and Life, Alan Lakein, Peter H. Wyden, Inc., 1973.

It's About Time! The Six Styles of Procrastination and How to Overcome Them, Linda Sapadin and Jack Maguire, Viking, 1996.

Making Time Work for You, Harold L. Taylor, Harold Taylor Time Consultants, 1998.

Take Time for Your Life, Cheryl Richardson, Broadway Books, 1998.

30 Days to a Simpler Life, Connie Cox and Cris Evatt, Plume, 1998.

Time Management for Unmanageable People, Ann McGee-Cooper and Duane Trammell, Bantam Books, 1994.

You Don't Have to Go Home From Work Exhausted, Ann McGee-Cooper and Duane Trammell, Bantam Books, 1992.

Time Management for the Creative Person, Lee Silber, Three Rivers Press, 1998.

SPACE

Children's Rooms, Jane Lott, Prentice-Hall, 1989.

The Complete Home Organizer, Maxine Ordesky, Grove Press, 1993.

The Family Manager's Guide for Working Moms, Kathy Peel, Ballantine Books, 1997.

Get Your Act Together, Pam Young and Peggy Jones, HarperPerennial, 1993.

Getting Organized, Stephanie Winston, Warner Books, 1978.

Home Offices and Workspaces, Sunset Books, Lane Publishing Company, 1986.

Making the Most of Storage, Debora Robertson, Rizzoli International, 1996.

Making the Most of Workspaces, Lorrie Mack, Rizzoli International, 1995.

Organized Closets and Storage, Stephanie Culp, Writer's Digest Books, 1990.

The Organized Executive, Stephanie Winston, Warner Books, 1983.

Organized to Be the Best, Susan Silver, Adams Hall, 1991.

Organizing from the Inside Out, Julie Morgenstern, Henry Holt, 1998.

Organizing Your Home Office for Success, Lisa Kanarek, Blakely Press, 1998.

Organizing Your Workspace, Odette Pollar, Crisp Publications, 1992.

Simply Organized, Connie Cox and Cris Evatt, Putnam Publishing Group, 1986.

Speed Cleaning, Jeff Campbell and The Clean Team, Dell Publishing, 1991.

Storage, Dinah Hall and Barbara Weiss, DK Publishing, 1997.

Taming the Office Tiger, Barbara Hemphill, Random House, 1996.

Taming the Paper Tiger, Barbara Hemphill, Random House, 1996.

Working from Home, Paul and Sarah Edwards, Jeremy P. Tarcher, Inc., 1990.

Working Solo, Terri Lonier, Portico Press, 1996.

GOAL-SETTING/INSPIRATION

Live the Life You Love, Barbara Sher, Dell Publishing, 1996.

Making a Living Without a Job, Barbara J. Winter, Bantam Books, 1993.

Take Yourself to the Top, Laura Berman, Fortgang, 1998.

Wishcraft, Barbara Sher, Ballantine Books, 1979.

Acknowledgments

My most heartfelt thanks goes to my extraordinary daughter, Jessi. You have been a partner in every page, by sacrificing time with me at a critical time in your life and by adding your editorial eye when needed. Your patience, generosity, and understanding during this process showed wisdom beyond your years. Most important, I thank you for filling every moment we have together with your extraordinary love, volumes of laughter, and wonderful perspective. You fill my life with meaning and your own very magical light.

This book would not have come into being without the significant contributions of an extraordinary team of people. I extend my deepest gratitude to John Sterling for being a visionary and believer in the *inside out* approach; David Sobel for being a brilliant editor, true advocate, and invaluable partner in the creation of this book; my agent, Faith Hamlin for providing wise and loving guidance and helping me grow as an author and a person; and Carol Crespo, for helping me get my words on the page and for filling the journey with laughter and delight. Thank you to Anne Geiger for your input on the manuscript, and Sean McCormack for your input *of* the manuscript.

A very special thanks to Nancy Peske whose talent and comprehensive eye helped us pull the various elements of the book together at the end to create a whole that is greater than the sum of its parts.

I am deeply appreciative to the magnificent team at Holt who support me in ways I could never have imagined: Maggie Richards, Elizabeth Shreve, Tracy Locke, Sarah Hutson, and Lisa Simmons. I also extend my deep gratitude to the remarkable people in the design and production department at Holt, whose stellar time management skills got this book delivered on time.

A lifetime of thanks to Valerie Soll, Deb Kinney, and Ron Young for your invaluable comments on the material for the book and for your long-term commitment and devotion to Task Masters, to me, and to helping people conquer chaos from the inside out.

Thanks also to Lori Marks, Marjorie Stein, and M. J. McConnell for contributing to the success of Task Masters and lending your skills and passion to the team.

Reams of appreciation go to my incredibly organized, linear/digital, visual/tactile assistant Karyn who arrived like a miracle in the middle of this writing project and instantly freed my mind and time to focus on the writing of the book.

Thank you to Jonathan Tisch who very generously shared his time, wisdom, and methods for managing his time from the inside out—which he's been doing for many, many years! And Kathy and Ed Harvey, for sharing their wisdom about working as a team with their kids.

This book would also not have been possible without the support of some extraordinary people who believe in my work and have helped me share it with the world. Thank you from the bottom of my heart to Oprah for so generously sharing her stage with me and helping me spread the word about working from the inside out throughout the world. Thank you to Terry Gross of *Fresh Air* for bringing my message to her listeners and conducting an unforgettable interview. Thanks to Marty Moss-Cohane of *Radio Times,* Nancy Jacoby of MSNBC, Donnabeth Cohen of *Later Today,* and Gerry Richman, Joe Garbarino, Niki Vettel, Erika Herman, Norbert Een, and Ann Herzog at PBS. I am grateful to all the journalists who think of me when writing about organization. Special thanks to Kim McCabe, Angie Kraus, Terry Goulder, Michael Torchiere, Naomi Person, Amy Salit, Danny Miller, Phyllis Myers, Gordon Rothman, Jonathan Welch, Ken Linde, Rebecca Herschkopf, Lisa Lee Freeman, Joe Terry, Carol Marten, Carol Cooper, and Steven Duvall for being true believers.

Thanks to Barbara Brennan for her unbridled enthusiasm and help in thinking BIG, to Michael Civin for helping put a shape on my business, to Urban Mulvehill for being there from the start with wise advice and genuine caring, to Alex Linden for helping me rise to the next level, to Suze Orman for so generously sharing her wisdom, to Judy Misset for sharing her experience, to Lisa LaVecchia for more than I can think of, and to Linda Jacobs for being an enabler in the most positive sense of the word.

Thank you from the bottom of my heart to all of my clients, seminar attendees, and thousands of readers for sharing your individual stories, challenges, and successes. Your generosity and honesty fuel my motivation and give my work true meaning.

A huge hug and eternal gratitude to Barbara Hemphill for paving the way in the organizing industry, and being an extraordinary mentor and friend.

Deep appreciation to Harry Lowenstein, Irwin Coplen, Ken Yancey, and Christine Goodno at SCORE for giving me a kick start and keeping me going through the years. Many thanks to all my colleagues at NAPO and NSA for inspiring, guiding and motivating me along the way.

For being there with love, support, and advice whenever I reach out, I thank my close friends Judy Wineman, Zoe Anderheggen, Ric Murphy, Jeff Neuman, Kathryn Grody, Terri Lonier, Valerie Soll, Camille and Peter Ehrenberg, and all of the Dermans, Driesens, Cohens, Sorras and Sporers.

And finally I thank my family for their consistent love and support: My parents David and Sonia (who also served as readers for the manuscript); Myra, Alberto, Amanda, Jasmin, and Adam (who love me no matter how infrequently I call); Rhonda (whose belief in me is a constant source of strength); Steve and Sue Morgenstern (who are my rocks of wisdom, calm, and laughter); Thelma and Bud Bayuk (who have been cheering me on all along); and to my mother-in-law Lillian Colon (who has become a good and cherished friend).

Index

About the Author

Julie Morgenstern is the Founder of Task Masters, a professional organizing company that provides consulting services to individuals and companies. Her corporate clients have included American Express, Sony Music, and Microsoft, among many others. In addition to her regular appearances on MSNBC's *The Home Page,* Julie is a frequent guest on many national television programs and a popular speaker around the country. She lives in New York City with her daughter.